Edge Innovation

Ben A. Ratje

300
Publishing

Praise for Edge Innovation

"Edge Innovation is the ultimate easy-to-understand and practical guide for generating great ideas fast. Highly recommended for business owners and their creative teams."

Andreas Hesse, Co-Licensor of the PUSH UP PRO and IRON GYM PUSH UP, with over 2,000,000 sold worldwide

"It won't take you long to find the extraordinary in this book. Turn a few pages and you'll soon find the secrets to creative thinking laid out before you."

Dr. B.C. Shine, CMO of CJ GROUP
Bestselling Author of Spinkre Insights

"If you want to know how to create great ideas faster than your competition, this is THE book to buy, read and apply."

Paul Cannon, Co-Creator, Mastermind Ideas Summit,
www.mastermindingideas.com

"Edge Innovation takes a fresh approach to getting creative that will build on what you already know, and leave you thirsting for more."

Duncan Cho, Senior Vice President of Marketing, KUMHO TIRES

"Here at TOZ our goal is to help our clients become more successful. One of the key factors to achieve that goal and grow from 1 to 21 branches in less than 10 years was innovation. If you want to master the skill of innovation, this book is one of the best resources you can find."

Y.H. Kim, CEO, TOZ

To Eunjung, my love

Published by 300 Publishing

Printed in the United States of America

Editing by Yoav Korn
Illustrations by Yoonique
Cover Design by 300 Publishing

ISBN 978-89-97411-05-4

Acknowledgements

Thank you to my wife Eunjung for constantly inspiring me and challenging me to do better. I love your eye for finding problems that others simply cannot see. It's a true gift for innovation.

Thank you to mom and dad, for instilling a CAN-do attitude in me and supporting me to start my first business.

Thank you to Ken for being a great mentor. You pushed me to start thinking more creatively and taking my business to Asia. You are never far from my thoughts.

Thank you to my business partner Peter Han for always pushing me to go that little bit further.

Thank you to my editor Yoav Korn. I can honestly say that without you this book wouldn't be as easy to read as it is now. You've helped me share my message in the best way.

Thank you to my friends and mentors who help me expand my own innovativeness. A special thanks to Dr. Shin, Dan, Woojung, Bill, Jeremy, Luke, Eunchul, Ulf, Haejin, Gwonjin, Dongjo, Unchung, Minkyung, and Mr. Oh.

Thank you to the global megacity of Seoul for offering millions of opportunities for me to discover new things.

Finally, a special thank you to all INFLUENCE7 team members, clients, associates and joint venture companies. Thanks to you we continue to help companies and professionals innovate and communicate better.

Contents

Part 2: The 4 Step to Innovation   89

Step 1: InnoTarget   93

Step 2: InnoTools   137

Step 3: InnoCreation   195

Introduction

Innovation is for a select few.

These select few are born with their ability to innovate; it's in their genes.

These selected few reap all the rewards: the money, the power, the ability to influence the world the way they want.

Or so, we are led to believe…

But is this fact or fiction?

Unfortunately lots of people believe it to be true.

And to some degree it probably is, with the EXCEPTION of the first part: Innovation is NOT for the select few NOR is it a genetic thing.

Most great innovators are not innovative by chance.

Sure there are some people who are naturally more talented than others when it comes to creativity, but their inborn talent can only get them so far.

Ultimately innovation is a skill that can be learned.

Steve Jobs is a 'learned' innovator.

So is Jeff Bezos, founder of amazon.com.

So too is Richard Branson, founder of over 200 Virgin companies.

And so are the Google founders, Sergey Brin and Larry Page.

A quick scan of any of their biographies will show you that none of these people were "born to innovate".

So you don't have to be either.

The answer to how many famous innovators have become innovative are hidden within the pages of this book.

I'd like you to believe that you too have the potential to become a world-renowned innovator.

This book is your guide to becoming more innovative. STARTING TODAY.

In this book, you will find the proven strategies that the world's greatest innovators have applied consistently to create great businesses, products and services.

All you have to do is learn these strategies and your chances of becoming an innovator (or a much better one) will increase dramatically.

I wrote this book because I found that even though there are many books written on innovation, most of them are truly IMPRACTICAL.

They are war stories from former executives of 'innovative' companies, that offer a good read but no specifics. And then there are books on creativity that are fun and ask you to do some exercises, but leave you with nothing to apply to real work when you finish reading them.

This book is different.

This book is as PRACTICAL as it gets and you will be able to easily apply what you learn to your work. You can use all or some of the tips in here to create new businesses, products, services, marketing strategies, innovative corporate strategies, and so on. It's also fun to read and there will be more than a few exercises to apply what you learn.

After reading, you will be able to create a new product or service from A to Z or update your current ones dramatically.

You will find this book to be an easy read. Don't be fooled though, reading alone will not make you more innovative.

What matters more is that you apply the simple Action Steps that you will find at the end of most chapters, and that you start living all of the principles you find in this book.

With that said, I'm confident that you will enjoy this book and learn lots of practical ideas. My greatest wish for you is to apply the principles you learn FAST and create businesses, products or services the world truly needs.

To your great innovation,

Ben A. Ratje

Seoul, South Korea

Part 1
The **Basics** of
Innovation

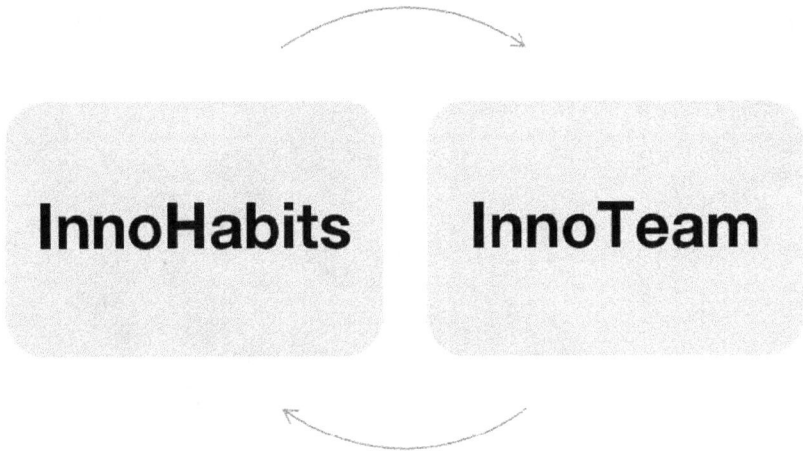

InnoHabits

InnoTeam

The Basics of Innovation

In this section you will be introduced to the Basics of Innovation.

The basics of innovation consist of two main areas: InnoHabits and InnoTeam.

In the InnoHabits chapters you will learn how to increase your creativity and innovativeness by learning a few simple activities that you can do on a daily basis.

In the InnoTeam chapters you will learn about the importance of a team, how to pick the right people and what your strong points for innovation are.

The focus is to make being creative and innovative a daily part of your life to the point that it comes very EASILY to you. You'll also learn how to surround yourself with people who will help you naturally create and innovate.

Are you ready to make innovation a part of your life?

Basic 1

InnoHabits

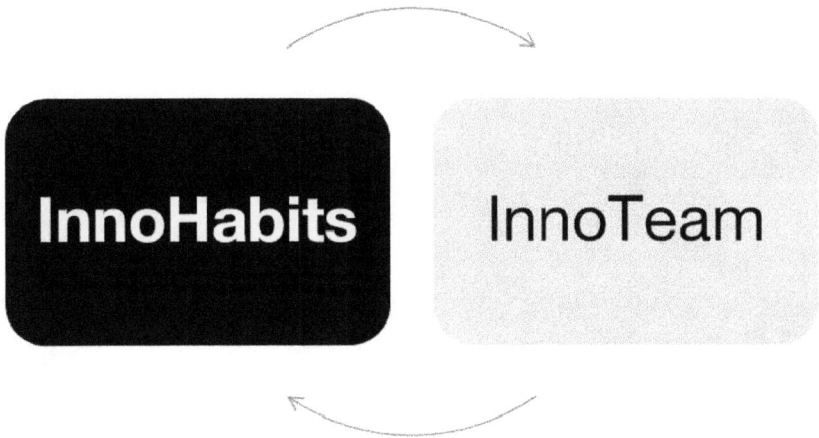

InnoHabits   InnoTeam

Why InnoHabits?!

The Problem in a Nutshell

When people think of innovative people, they think that these people were born with the "creative spark". And if being creative and innovative is a trait a person is born with, how can it ever be learned?

But in reality that's NOT the case (though there are clearly some exceptions).

The Purpose of InnoHabits

> The purpose of InnoHabits is to help you become more innovative and creative NATURALLY.

Most innovative people are more innovative than others, not only because they THINK differently but also because they DO differently.

Being innovative is easy for them because of certain HABITS which they practice DAILY.

Becoming more creative and innovative is for the most part a learnable skill.

In this part of the book, you will learn how to get to the same level of creativity and innovation.

Imagine that being creative and innovative comes easily to you...

If you apply what you learn in this chapter, it will.

When to Use InnoHabits

What's written in this part of the book should be used at least to a small degree on a DAILY basis.

It's the foundation (=basis) of all creativity and innovation. In some way it's the fast way for you to easily come up with more and better ideas. You can make or break your creativity based on whether or not you apply the activities in this chapter.

But don't worry: they're all easy and fun to apply. So doing one thing differently as suggested in this part will mostly (though not always) be effortless.

Get ready to build up your InnoBasics and NATURALLY become more innovative!

Be an Entrepreneur First

What is Steve Jobs first: an entrepreneur or an innovator?

An entrepreneur!

What is Bill Gates first: an entrepreneur or an innovator?

An entrepreneur!

What are the founders of Google first: entrepreneurs or innovators?

Entrepreneurs!

When you look at most successful innovators in history, you will soon find that they were entrepreneurs first.

Nowadays, designers lay claim to innovation because of what a product LOOKS like.

It used to be that inventors laid claim to innovation because of what they INVENTED.

I would suggest to you that entrepreneurs lay claim to innovation, because they create a product not based on whether it looks good or not (though ideally it should look good) nor do they focus mainly on the product invention itself, instead they focus on whether a product will become SUCCESSFUL or not.

What are the big differences between designers, inventors and entrepreneurs? Let's have a quick look at the following table to understand some of the differences:

	Designers	Inventors	Entrepreneurs
What they focus on	• Creating products that LOOK nice • DESIGNING products until they look stylish	• Creating products THEY like • Unintentionally making it non-user friendly	• Making a profit • Creating products clients NEED
What they spend their time on	• By themselves in their "designer zone" • Try their best to make their product look good	• By themselves in their "inventor zone" • Working ON the product day and night	• With the client asking questions • Doing market research to determine clients' unmet needs
Their ultimate goal	• Winning an award at the design fair • Hearing someone tell them "WOW! That looks cool! Great design!"	• The product itself	• Happy clients • Earning lots of money because of the great product /service created

An innovation success can be measured not by what it looks like but by the unmet need it fills or the problem it solves for the end user (and of course by how many people buy it and how much money it makes).

Hence, the clear winner in the innovation challenge are entrepreneurs.

Again, you want to be an entrepreneur first.

Let's take Bill Gates for example. Why did he become so successful? Because he was a programmer or because he was an entrepreneur?

Of course Bill Gates is also a great programmer (though some might disagree with me here), but the real reason he became so famous is because of his ENTREPRENEURIAL skill.

Microsoft became so big, so fast not because it had the best software, but because young Bill Gates got the biggest deal with IBM in the history of computers at that time (by being an entrepreneur first). Some people say that the initial software was not even fully developed by Microsoft - again he was an entrepreneur first.

The point is that there were lots of other software companies in the late 70s and early 80s, but it was Bill Gates who came out on top and is one of the few titans who we remember. He did this by making the right deals and hiring the right people.

Of course his vision for personal computers mattered, but he didn't focus on sitting in his basement working on the software only; he also spent time on thinking and acting like an entrepreneur.

The same should be true for you.

You can be a great inventor and designer, but remember you are only one person.

An entrepreneur can make connections with people and other resources that many inventors and designers often fail to utilize.

You can afford to lose every person on the team, except the entrepreneur!

The entrepreneur is the one who *finds* the idea (not always the one who comes up with it), who finds the right people and who (in some cases) finds the deals and resources to make the idea successful.

Be an entrepreneur first!

Great innovators are great entrepreneurs first. Nothing beats entrepreneurial thinking in the world of innovation, neither inventive thinking nor design thinking.

Innovation into Action

Compare ENTREPRENEURS with inventors and designers. Think about Richard Branson or Steve Jobs or Bill Gates and write down 10 characteristics that make them great entrepreneurs or that give them a strong advantage in creating innovations in comparison to inventors and designers:

1. _____
2. _____
3. _____
4. _____
5. _____
6. _____
7. _____
8. _____
9. _____
10. _____

Use Your Brain!

Are you using your brain fully?

To become innovative you need to use your brain and there are certain ways to make your brain work for – and not against – you when you're coming up with new ideas. Let's have a look at some of them:

1. Use your WHOLE brain

This probably isn't news to most of you but, just in case, I thought you ought to know that your brain is split into two equal halves!

Just as you have a right and a left hand, you have a right brain and a left brain.

And even though they may look the same, each side is in charge of completely opposite things. Each side is as important as the other. And you need to use each side to become truly creative.

Here's a list of what each side is in charge of:

Left Brain	Right Brain
• Rationality	• Intuition
• Logic	• Creativity
• Words	• Pictures
• Part Thinking	• Holistic Thinking
• Science	• Art
• Right hand	• Left hand

Current thinking says that your right brain is in charge of innovation, but this is in fact NOT true.

Innovation needs a combination of both your left and right brain. You cannot innovate using only one side of your brain. For you to become truly innovative, you need to develop BOTH sides of your brain.

Einstein said it best: 'Innovation is not the product of logical thought, although the result is tied to logical structure."

What he means is that you need NON-logical thought (right brain) and a logical structure (left brain) to come up with a great innovation.

Use both your sides of your brain!

2. Give your brain a break

How did Newton discover the law of gravity? While working hard on the problem or while taking a break under a tree? As most of you probably know, it happened while he was taking a break.

How about the famous word "Eureka!"? Was Archimedes working hard on the problem when he figured out how to measure the volume of an irregular object or was he taking a break in the bath tub?. It happened, rather famously, in the tub.

Einstein was famous for taking breaks when he couldn't come up with the solution to a problem. Often he would pick up his violin and play for a while.

Our brains work very well to come up with great ideas, but only if we give them enough breaks in between (and those are often the times when the best ideas pop into your head).

You also might want to consider taking a power nap after lunch. According to Lothar Seiwert, Germany's leading time management expert, a power nap after lunch improves performance by 35% and increases the ability to make the correct decisions by 50%.

Take a break!

3. Give your brain pressure

Interestingly, our brains often come up with great ideas when put under pressure.

When forced to come up with great ideas, we often do.

Think in terms of deadlines for your boss or another authority figure. When put under pressure our brains come up with and develop great ideas fast.

When working on your next project give yourself a deadline you cannot change under any circumstances. This will give you the incentive to come up with new ideas or solutions to your problem.

This idea gels well with our current understanding of stress.

Pressure works as long as it's based on good stress. Stress experts call this *eustress* (*eu* is the Greek prefix meaning well or good). Experts also say that eustress can give you a competitive edge when working on something. For example, professional sportsmen are often under eustress which makes them perform better.

How do you know if the stress you're experiencing is positive? Even the body cannot differentiate between eustress and its evil twin *distress*, you can determine it by taking a look at what you're working on. If it's something that you usually like to do or is a challenge to a goal you want to achieve it's probably eustress.

If on the other hand the stress comes from the outside and you don't want to do something that gives you stress, chances are high it's distress.

Choosing your own challenges will pretty much guarantee you experience eustress, so focus on that for your next project.

4. Give your brain water

Water.

Our brain needs it. But we often don't drink it (or not enough of it at any rate).

It is estimated that to function well, we need to drink a minimum of 3 liters of water each and every single day – depending on which doctor you ask it may even be up to 4 liters per day. Unfortunately most of us fail to do so.

Doctors say that during the average day the human body loses approximately 2½ liters of water, meaning we should take in at least that amount, if not more.

When we don't drink enough water we become DEHYDRATED.

DEHYDRATION instantly effects the brain. Symptoms include headaches, dizziness and a general feeling of tiredness (even though you've gotten your full 6 -8 hours of sleep).

To avoid dehydration, and to ensure your brain operates well, do yourself a favor and drink enough water every day!

5. Give your brain new neuron-connections

Your brain consist of about 100 billion neurons which are connected via synapses.

Neurons are cells in our brain that specialize in carrying messages through our brain. Neurons basically allow human beings to think and remember things.

It is estimated that our brain creates about a million new connections every second of our lives.

Neurons connect the left brain and the right brain. Neurons create as many connections as we allow them to.

To become more creative, you need to increase your neurons and the connections between these neurons (also called 'neuron-connections').

Every time you apply any of the strategies in the rest of this book your neuron-connections will increase more swiftly than normal. As a result you will become more and more creative.

If you check the level of neuron-connections in the average person's brain, you will see a forest of neuron-connections.

But if you look at the brain of a highly creative person, you will see a teeming jungle of neuron-connections.

Increase you neuron-connections to increase your creativity (you will learn more on how to do that in the next part of this book).

6. Give your brain physical activity

As with water, your brain functions far better if you exercise regularly.

Even though our brains can function without our bodies, they are both intimately connected. Working out will also increase your brain's capacity to function well and ultimately bring you better ideas that can lead to better innovations.

German fitness guru and bestselling author Dr. Ulrich Strunz suggests walking or jogging (slowly) daily to stir up creativity. Jogging stimulates the production of the hormone ACTH in our body.

ACTH is also known as the creativity hormone, so get jogging to get creative!

7. Give your brain a problem, and let it come up with a solution

Your brain is an answer-giving machine. If you give it a problem it will come up with multiple solutions.

In his wonderful book 'The Success Principles', bestselling author Jack Canfield explains that our brains use something called RAS (Reticular Activating System) to help us achieve our goals faster.

What the RAS also does is help you solve problems faster and smarter.

The easiest way to activate your brain is to constantly focus on a problem you'd like to solve or a goal you'd like to achieve.

Great Innovators know how to use their brains. They treat their brains well and use them to their utmost capacity.

Innovation into Action

List 3 things you can do to make your brain more effective.

1. _____

2. _____

3. _____

Use Your Senses!

"To draw you must close your eyes and sing."

Pablo Picasso

One of the things you need to master in order to become more creative is how to use your 3 main senses: seeing, listening, touching.

These are also the 3 primary ways that we as human beings learn. They can be summarized with the famous and widely used acronym VAP (Visual, Auditory, Practical).

To master creativity and innovation it is good to have a general understanding of all three, and especially about practical tips on how to stimulate them.

Visual Sense

You can stimulate your visual sense in two ways: seeing and reading. Also, your visual sense is highly stimulated by moving pictures and especially colors.

Here are a few things you can use to stimulate your visual sense:

Post-its: Use colored post-its to write down your ideas and put them up all over the wall, on your board, or simply to clarify or order your ideas on the table in front of you.

Many marketers, advertisers, trainers and presenters write down their ideas on post-its and then re-shuffle them until they find the perfect order. You can and should do the same.

Colors: Use colors for everything you do. Use colored paper. Use colored pens. Use colorful objects. The more colors you use, the more your right brain will be stimulated.

Pictures: Use pictures to get a clear idea of what you're working on. If you're trying to innovate new packaging for your product, get lots of pictures and images of existing product packaging.

Movies: Use movies, TV and videos (educational only please) to learn about certain products, services or industries that you are innovating on. If you see someone else doing it, talking about it, and sharing their story, chances are higher you can learn about that area faster.

Drawing: Instead of writing down your ideas and concepts, try drawing them. You don't even need to be good at it. Drawing is NOT only for skilled artists! The main thing is that you give your right brain an opportunity to activate itself by thinking in images and putting them on paper.

Write down an idea for your business or product or service right now. Afterwards try drawing the idea out in the box below:

Idea: _____

Auditory Sense

You can stimulate your auditory senses in two ways: listening and speaking. Your auditory sense is stimulated by sounds you or others make.

Here are a few tips on how to activate it:

Music: Play music in the background while you're working with your team on new innovation projects. Music stimulates the mind (especially your right brain). Choose different music, depending on the mood you're trying to generate. Play active music, if you want to energize your team. Play relaxing music (e.g. Mozart) to put the team in a more relaxed state.

Einstein was famous for playing his violin every time he wasn't able to find a solution to a problem he was working on.

Talk: Talk with someone else about your ideas, your thoughts or problems you're trying to solve. Not only will you gain valuable feedback, but by verbalizing your thoughts, you will gain a deeper understanding of what it is you're trying to achieve. You may even come up with more ideas.

Melody: Sing ideas to yourself using the melodies of songs you like. That way ideas will stick in your mind longer and be easier to remember.

Voice Recorder: Speak your thoughts and ideas into a voice recorder and listen to it later on your mp3 player or in your car to stir up new ideas.

Practical Sense

You can stimulate your practical sense in two ways: touching and feeling. Your practical sense responds best to actually "doing it".

Here are a few specific tips on how to best activate it:

Real Objects: If you want to innovate a new cell phone get as many real cell phones in front of you as possible. Look at them. Touch them. Compare them. Do the same with products you want to combine with your new cell phone.

Real Experience: If you need to understand your target users, go out and meet them. To experience the taste of a product, try it. To experience why your clients have a certain problem, get the real experience and feel how they feel.

3x5 Cards: Summarize your ideas and findings on 3x5 cards, carry them with you at all times and review them regularly. The simple act of touching and going through the cards, helps you remember the real experience and come up with more ideas.

Innovative people use the above tips in some way every day.

Yesterday for example I used post-its to plan out a 2-hour seminar that needed improving; I had a meeting and drew out my ideas using 3 different color markers to make it visually more memorable; I listened to music to stimulate my mind while working on a new book I plan to write, and I visited one new location for online videos we're planning to film soon to get the "feel" of the place.

All these things may seem trivial, but ultimately they're the things that make people more creative when continuously used.

The best way to become more creative is by practicing a good mix of all the 3 senses simultaneously.

This way your brain will work at full-speed and chances are higher that you can come up with the next winning business idea.

Innovation into Action

Think of ways in which you can practically apply each of the three areas (visual, auditory, practical) to your daily tasks to make both the tasks and you more creative.

Visual: _____

Auditory: _____

Practical: _____

Impossible is Everything!

"It always seems impossible until it's done."

Nelson Mandela

"You can't do that!" or "That's impossible!" are the words most people don't like to hear. They are afraid of these words. They fear them more than hearing "You are stupid."

Not so for great innovators.

Great innovators are motivated, even inspired, by the words "You can't do that!" or "That's impossible!"

Great innovators believe that the word '"impossible" is EVERYTHING.

If no one says that word, they often believe that their idea is too small or too unimportant to be created. The word "impossible" gives innovators the motivation to push forward and show the world that it is in fact possible.

Think of some of the great products and services we now enjoy.

Weren't they "impossible" at first?

And yet, it's the things most people think is impossible that have the greatest value and impact on humankind once they're made possible.

For example, think back 20 years and imagine someone told you that you can call your pizzeria, order your favorite pizza and have it at your front door in 30 minutes or less.

Most of us would have said that that's impossible.

Yet, Domino's pizza made it possible and actually changed the entire takeout world.

I personally get a little annoyed if ANY home delivery food isn't there within 30 minutes. It doesn't matter if it's pizza or chicken or Chinese, Domino's has set a standard I expect all other take-out restaurants to follow.

Here's another example: think back to about 5 years ago and imagine someone told you that we will soon have super-thin mp3 players that you can hardly feel in your pocket, that have a screen to play movies and are super-small as well.

Again most of us would have said that's impossible.

Yet, APPLE made it possible with their iPod nano, and again added more value to millions of mp3 users around the globe.

That's what I'm talking about when I say "Impossible is Everything".

Impossible should be your inspiration and motivation for creating a killer product or service.

Great innovators let themselves be guided by the word "impossible". They turn impossible into possible. They know that impossible is Everything.

Great Innovators turn "impossible" into "possible".

What is currently impossible in your industry or your field?

Innovation into Action

Write down something in your field which is widely regarded as impossible.

_____

Now write down several ways you could solve this 'impossible' problem:

_____

_____

_____

_____

_____

Creativity Comfort Zone

"To the degree we're not living our dreams, our comfort zone has more control of us than we have over ourselves."

Peter McWilliams

Have you ever heard about the story of the zoo lion?

There was once a lion that got caught in the wild while still a cub. The cub was sold and brought via ship to a newly opened zoo in Europe.

For the next 5 years the lion lived in the zoo, growing up more like a house cat than a real lion in a 20 x 20 meter cage.

Then, one day a rich visitor came to the zoo. Seeing the lion, she thought what a pity it was that the poor lion had to live in such a small cage.

She talked with the owner of the zoo and asked about the lion's story, and discovered that he had never been free in his entire life.

The rich lady asked the owner how much she had to pay to free the lion and send him back to Africa. Within 10 minutes she had all the rights for the lion. Within 1 week the lion was back in Africa, traveling there with the rich lady and a team of locals to support her.

When the team arrived in the wild, and the lion was finally set free, the lady noticed something really strange: even though the lion was now free, it only moved within an area of 20 x 20 meters, as if he was still in the zoo.

When she asked the people in the car who helped her to bring the lion back what happened, they calmly answered:

'Though his body is free, his mind is not. His comfort zone is 20 x 20 meters. It will take him a long time to break free of his mental cage.'

The same is unfortunately true for most people!

They live in the 'cage of their own mind'. They are caught in their own little worlds.

Most people eat the same type of food every day, meet the same type of people every day, and spend their time in the same areas every day. They drive the same kind of car for the rest of their lives and live in the same neighborhoods.

Several of my fellow students from high school rarely leave Germany. They go for an occasional trip to Spain in summer, but that's it. Even traveling around Germany is discomforting for some of them.

Many people I met in Canada and the US have never left their home countries. Many of them have not even been to many cities in the US (If you haven't already guessed, traveling is just one example how to get out of your comfort zone).

And at the end of the day, they're all asking themselves: Why am I not creative?

Most people who work in big companies stay in their departments.

Marketing people stick with marketing people. Accountants with accountants, executives with executives, and so on.

If these people met people from other departments (i.e. stepped out of their comfort zones), they would discover that there's a lot to learn from people from other departments.

Different thoughts. Different ideas. Different points of view.

All this could lead to better ideas for the company, but unfortunately most people don't change their routines, because of their comfort zones.

> # Most people live in their comfort zones until the day they die.

A little exercise that we do with participants during our Innovation workshops is called 'City Comfort Zone'.

We ask participants to mark on their city's subway map all the areas they travel to in an average month. Surprisingly most people have what my business partner Peter Han calls the 'Comfort Triangle'.

Most people move from job to home to one other place. They keep going to the same 3 locations again and again, never leaving their comfort zones.

Strangely enough, the people who visit the most different locations are usually also the most creative (often with the more creative jobs, or the ones in higher positions because of their creative ideas).

They often try new foods, meet new people, visit new places and events and usually are more excited and happier with their lives than other participants.

So, what's stopping you from being creative?

Well…I have news for you:

> # It's your comfort zone that stops you from being more creative and innovative!

To become more creative you have to constantly get out of your comfort zone. The most creative people on the planet have much larger comfort zones than the average person.

They constantly challenge themselves to step out of their comfort zones. They constantly go beyond their beliefs and their current thinking of what is possible in their business and industry. They try new things and reap not some, but lots and lots of rewards.

Do people who constantly step out of their comfort zones usually enjoy it? Usually not. Just like everyone else they are sometimes not so thrilled. Stepping out of your comfort zone means becoming first and foremost 'uncomfortable'.

You can substitute the word 'uncomfortable' for afraid, worried, uncertain, etc.

© yoonique

People who constantly step out of their comfort zones have learned one lesson though: everything new usually feels uncomfortable at first, but after a short period that discomfort turns into comfort and joy.

Take for example your first day at your new job. It was probably quite uncomfortable, right? New people, new work system, new boss, (maybe) new industry, and new rules to follow.

Thinking about the first day at their new job usually doesn't engender the greatest feeling of joy for most people.

But after a short while of learning and connecting with coworkers, they feel more and more comfortable in their new jobs.

The same is true for the rest of your comfort zones.

Everything new feels uncomfortable at first.

But the more you do it, the more comfortable you will get and the larger your comfort zone becomes.

And every time you step out of your comfort zone you learn something new (i.e. new ideas).

The more new things you learn, the more ideas you come up with, and coming up with more ideas is what defines the creative and innovative person.

Great innovators constantly get out of their comfort zones. They don't enjoy it but they do it anyway, and reap all the rewards.

Innovation into Action

What are 3 things you can do to step out of your comfort zone this week?

1. _____   Date:_____

2. _____   Date:_____

3. _____   Date:_____

Make More Mistakes

"I have not failed. I've just found 10,000 ways that won't work."

Thomas A. Edison

How often did Edison fail before he invented the light bulb?

How often did Henry Ford fail (and drive his engineers crazy) before the V8 motor was created?

How often did the Wright Brothers almost kill themselves before they got airborne.

You're probably thinking: A LOT!!!

There's an exercise related to making mistakes that I learned from one of Tim Brown's (CEO of IDEO) presentations. It goes like this:

He put people in pairs and asks them to introduce themselves to the other person.

He then asked them to draw the other person to the best of their ability within 1 minute.

Afterwards he asked them to exchange their drawings.

Can you guess what the first word is that came out of almost everybody's mouth?

"I'm sorry for my bad drawing!!!"

The first thing people did was say sorry.

36

When giving children the same exercise, what do you think they do? Do you think their first words are 'I'm sorry'?

No, they're not!

Children (in the beginning at least) draw far worse than adults, but they don't say sorry.

The lesson behind this is of course that as grown-ups we are afraid of making mistakes or looking stupid. We are afraid of trying something new and looking stupid. We are afraid of not being perfect.

Children are not afraid. They are used to making mistakes.

The simple lesson I want you to remember from this is:

Make More Mistakes! (MMM)

And making more mistakes (and learning from them of course) leads to the 2nd meaning of MMM: Make More Money!

If you want to become more creative, innovative and even successful, you have to make more mistakes.

You have to try several ways that don't work before you can find the one that does.

Creativity means coming up with new, great ideas. But in order to find that 1 great idea, you will probably end up creating 100 that stink.

And that's OK!

It's just part of the creative and innovative process. That's why it is so important that you get used to making mistakes. Don't give up after the first mistake. Make more.

The mistakes you make usually give you the clues you need to create that one great innovation. If you don't follow this process, chances are you might not come up with that great idea at all.

Whenever I start creating a new workshop, I test it like crazy.

I test it on people I meet, I test it by delivering short presentations on the topic, and I test it by giving shorter seminars before doing longer workshops.

Even though I've been doing this for years, have gotten highest ratings for my programs and am often asked by others to help improve their training programs, do you think my programs are perfect form the start? Of course not!

I keep testing and making more mistakes until they are.

Do you think they could have gotten that way without all these mistakes?

Not a chance!

And I believe the same is true of any other product or service you want to create.

Billionaire Ross Perot probably said it best: *"Punishing honest mistakes stifles creativity. I want people moving and shaking the earth and they're going to make mistakes."*

Great innovators make more mistakes!

Innovation into Action

In which areas do you think you need to make mistakes faster, learn faster and make progress faster? Remember: great products and services come from great mistakes.

_____

_____

_____

Try Something New!

"I like my job because it involves learning. I like being around smart people who are trying to figure out new things. I like the fact that if people really try they can figure out how to invent things that actually have an impact."

Bill Gates

One of the easiest ways to increase your creativity is to try something that you've never tried before.

And I'm not just talking about crazy things here, like skydiving, eating frog's legs or swimming with sharks (although these are options).

I'm talking about things that you can virtually do every single day. Things that often take no extra time (or a little, but trust me, you will have a lot of fun doing them).

A few years ago, I visited a global conference, here in Seoul, South Korea.

One of the seminars was about creativity and innovation. Two global innovation experts gave a presentation on the topic.

During the Q & A session, I asked both of them to give the audience 3 practical tips on how to increase their creativity in their daily lives.

I got blank stares.

The speakers needed to move to the next question first, before they could answer mine (they needed more time to think).

The answer that came from both was simple: Try something new! They gave a few examples of new things to try, but that was it.

Even though I was a little disappointed that both gave the same answer, I was again confirmed about the importance of trying new things to increase your creativity.

Trying new things broadens your perspective and gives you new ideas. And for creativity and innovation, there is almost nothing more important than that.

> # To become more innovative you should try something new daily.

Here is a list of 10 tips to help you along:

Tip #1: Try a new area

Most people stay in their own neighborhoods or their own cities or their own countries their entire lives. Why not try a new place and become a "discoverer".

<u>Try visiting a new area in your city</u>

Many people stay in their neighborhoods, near their workplaces and/or near downtown most of the time.

Break out of it!

Try to visit the richest neighborhood, then the poorest, then the one furthest away, then the one you would never visit (as long as it's not dangerous).

Visit the best food area, the best party area, the best area for recreation, the university area, etc.

Visit areas in your city that you've never visited before. If you live in a small town, try visiting another town or city nearby.

Try visiting a new nature spot

When was the last time you visited the zoo, went to the beach or climbed a mountain?

You could also visit a park nearby your home or office whenever the pressure gets too much.

All this will lead to new experiences and new ideas.

I once read that IBM engineers use this very tip. When IBM engineers run out of ideas to solve their business problems, they visit the zoo, watch the animals, and reportedly often get the idea for solving their problem outside their office.

If it works for them, why not for you?

Try traveling to a new country

Which countries have you visited?

Studies show that most people don't travel much. The main reason is fear of the new culture, and especially language. Another reason is that people think traveling is too expensive.

Don't let that stop you!

Start traveling. There are neighboring countries (or states) that are easy and inexpensive to travel to. No need to go for 2 weeks. A short 3-5 day trip will usually give you all the benefits you seek.

Meet people. Talk. Taste different food. Visit new locations. Check out shopping malls. Do anything that's new.

If you want to have some 'practical fun', check out all the product and service innovations the countries have to offer and think about how to apply them to your place of work in your country.

Tip #2: Try a new media

We all watch TV and movies, listen to music, and read books and magazines. Yet, how often do we try something new?

Here are a couple of things you should try:

If you like horror movies, try comedies.

If you like action, try romance.

If you like jazz, try hard rock.

If you like hip hop, try classical.

If you like pop, try folk.

If you read fashion magazines, try science.

If you read investment magazines, try sports.

If you read novels, try business books.

If you read cooking books, try philosophy.

There's a whole world of media out there to try out and enjoy. Get your ideas flowing by exposing yourself to a new area you haven't tried yet.

Tip #3: Try a new food

When was the last time you tried a new food or a new beverage (out of choice I mean)?

Too many people eat the same, drink the same and go to the same type of restaurant all year long for the rest of their lives.

For example, if they visit a coffee shop, most people's pattern looks like this:

Monday:	Americano
Tuesday:	Americano
Wednesday:	Americano
Thursday:	Americano
Friday:	Americano
Saturday:	Americano
Sunday:	Americano

Wow, what a creative week!!!

Here is your week if you try something new:

Monday:	Americano
Tuesday:	Caramel Macchiato
Wednesday:	Iced Chai Latte
Thursday:	Americano
Friday:	Strawberry Smoothie
Saturday:	Perrier Lime Water
Sunday:	Americano

Can you see a pattern? I'm not saying give up your favorite (Americano). All I'm saying is try something new half of the time or at least 20% of the time.

Try it out for a week and see what happens.

This surely is one of the easiest ways to try something new.

It's so easy, because we have to eat and drink something at least 3 times a day.

Next time you go grocery shopping, try filling half of your shopping cart with food items you've never tried before.

If you always go for one particular brand of a certain food, try another brand.

If you always buy mainly meat, buy mainly veggies.

If you prefer sweet, try salty.

Next time you go to your regular coffee shop or restaurant try a new item you haven't had yet.

© yoonique

Also, give it a shot and try out some of the following restaurants if you haven't done so already: Mexican, Chinese, Korean, German, French, Italian (choose neither the regular pizzas or pastas, try something new), Arabic, Japanese, Spanish, Indian, British, Australian, Russian, Polish, the list is endless!

When you go out to eat, visit places where the owner comes from that country and ask what nationals would order to increase the authenticity of your experience. Many dishes are adjusted to the taste of the new country, but every restaurant always has a few original dishes. Ask for them!

The focus here is not that you always eat something that you like (most times you will, sometimes you won't), but to extend your comfort zone!

If you want to take your creativity to the next level, try the restaurants from the list above that most 'surprised' you.

Tip #4: Try a new store

Tomorrow, after work, visit a store you've never been to. If you're single, visit a baby shop pretending you're a parent or grandparent.

If you're older, visit some hip, cool places that teenagers and youngsters go to.

If you're young, visit your grandmother's favorite shop.

When you're in the shop, look around, talk with the people working there, ask questions about their products and pretend to be the ideal shopper who would go there (that's what many great innovators also do when they research a target group for a product they create).

It will seem weird at first, but the more you try it, the more you will get comfortable in ANY situation.

Whenever I need new ideas, I tend to go to shops that I usually don't go to much or that always have new and interesting products. It simply stirs up new ideas to solve my own creative problems.

Tip #5: Try to meet new people

Meet new people. Go to networking events. Go to trade shows. Go to events. Go to clubs you have never visited.

I once went to an investment group by mistake. And I can tell you that little mistake made a big difference not only in my financial life but in my life as a whole.

Also, due to my work as a trainer and consultant I meet a lot of different people from various jobs and industries.

I remember that once I got lots of tips from staff of a 'female-dominated' company. All my workshop participants were mothers and what was the topic of lunch? Their kids' education.

Trust me, I learned more in one hour about their problems as mothers making the right decision to educate their kids than I could have from spending a year trying to study the topic.

Get ideas from different people.

I will spend more time explaining this in detail in the next chapter.

Tip #6: Try a new product

Next time you buy new toiletries, home products or other types of products, choose a product or brand that you've never tried before.

For example for your washroom, I want you to buy a different shampoo, different soap, different toothbrush, different deodorant and so on.

The reason being is to stimulate your senses. Your sense of smell is one of your least trained senses.

Get used to different smells by simply changing all the products you use in your washroom.

You can easily apply this tip to all sorts of products you use a lot. Try something new!

Tip #7: Try a new mode of transportation

Most people always use the same mode of transportation.

This week, switch things up!

If you always get to work by car, try the bus or going by bicycle (if possible). Try the subway. Try rollerblades. Try those new mini-bikes.

My suggestion is also that if you're driving an average or above average car, go to a luxury car dealer and test drive one of their cars for a day. If you drive a luxury car, test drive an average car.

A friend of mine always takes a long bike ride to work. He once told me that by doing so he gets lots of ideas for his job and the problems he needs to solve. He also said that if he took his car into work (occasionally he does), he wouldn't come up with half his ideas.

Also, most people go to work and back home using the exact same route.

For once, try taking a different route home, if it takes you a little longer, that's OK. The benefit it can have on your brain and your creativity will have been worth it.

Tip #8: Try a new clothing style

Do you always wear suits? Try jeans and a T-Shirt.

Do you always wear jeans and a T-Shirt? Try suits.

Do you always dress sexy? Try conservative.

Do you always dress conservative? Try sexy.

How a person dresses can tell you a lot about that person (women understand this far better than most men).

Chances are high that the people around you wear similar clothing styles to you. To get a new perspective, try new clothes.

Maybe you can remember the first time you tried on a suit. Didn't you feel different? Didn't the people around you treat you differently when you wore your suit?

Try different styles and see how people around you respond. Each style will give you a new perspective and new ideas.

I used to wear big suits with a tie 95% of the time. Even on the weekends you would often find me wearing them, because I wanted to look professional.

It wasn't until I met a new friend that I changed my mind. He suggested that I try to wear more fitted suits and handkerchiefs instead of ties (or both) to look more fashionable.

At first, I was concerned that losing the tie and trying a tighter suit wasn't the right thing to do to, but later on it paid off. I got great compliments from all the people around me, those who knew me and those who had only just met me for the first time.

Later I changed to a more casual style by changing suit pants to jeans. I started mixing and matching styles. Ever since, my creativity has spiked, because I had learned more about the rules of the fashion industry.

There's a whole world of fashion out there and trust me it's exciting to learn from it.

Tip #9: Try a new response

Next time someone asks you 'How are you?' Give him or her a different response than usual.

If you always answer 'fine' try 'awesome' or 'terrific' for a change.

When someone asks you what you had for dinner and you usually give a short answer, try a long answer.

Try different responses in your day-to-day conversations.

Every response gets a reply. Yet different responses get different replies. See what different replies you can elicit.

Here in Korea, people don't ask each other "How are you?" a lot.

In my first year in Korea, I used to greet everyone I met with "Haeng-bok-hae-yo?" which means "Are you happy?" and is a very weird question here as much as it is in most countries to ask a stranger you've just met.

But instead of getting weird looks, it got everyone I talked to laughing and put them in a better state of mind. I greeted everyone from waiters to cashiers at the 7-11 to people I did business with, the same way.

The response was surprising and fantastic. Many people started remembering me whenever they saw me, simply because I had changed the way I greeted people (the fact that it was a little strange in a positive way also helped).

Tip #10: Try a new seat

When people come to a seminar or a meeting or a class or a workshop, they tend to sit in the same seat.

We have been conditioned to this behavior since elementary school (for some people since kindergarten), where we weren't supposed to sit in a different seat, so our teacher could remember our names.

Unfortunately in terms of creativity and innovation it has brought us a bad habit: always looking at things from the same perspective.

Some people always sit in the back (usually to hide). Some people always sit in the front. Some people always sit in the middle. Some people always sit on the right side. Some people always sit on the left side.

The easiest way to get multiple perspectives is by constantly changing your position and the way you look at something.

Next time you go to a meeting or seminar, try to sit somewhere you usually wouldn't.

Doing this habitually will lead to the following:

1. You'll find it easier to see ANYTHING from a different perspective.

2. You'll find it easier to look at your own business problems from different perspectives.

3. You'll find it easier to come up with different solutions for the problems you face.

Innovative people can see a problem from multiple perspectives, and they train themselves in this skill by sitting in different places.

Innovation into Action

What are 10 new things from that you could try out this month?

1. _____   Date:_____

2. _____   Date:_____

3. _____   Date:_____

4. _____   Date:_____

5. _____   Date:_____

6. _____   Date:_____

7. _____   Date:_____

8. _____   Date:_____

9. _____   Date:_____

10. _____   Date:_____

Talk to Someone You Do NOT Agree With

"When I disagree with a rational man, I let reality be our final arbiter; if I am right, he will learn; if I am wrong, I will; one of us will win, but both will profit."

Ayn Rand

One of the greatest keys to coming up with new ideas is to talk to people who you actually do NOT agree with.

Yes, you've read correctly.

I want you to talk with people you don't agree with.

Again, to become more creative you need to get out of your comfort zone and gain different perspectives.

Do you always ask the same people for advice? Do you always get the same answers?

One of the easiest ways to get a completely differently perspective is to talk to someone who in general does NOT think like you do.

Asking the same type of people will always give you the same type of response. To get new ideas for your creative problems at work, you need to ask others (often people who disagree with you).

For example, whenever I finish one of my books, I give it to 2 friends who in many ways do NOT agree with me. One doesn't like my writing style. And the other is not interested in business or self development books at all.

But because we are friends, they are willing to have a look. After they read, I shut up, ready to listen and ready to take their feedback.

Even though it is often painful, I write down everything they tell me. Out of these conversations I get the most amazing insights and (hopefully) write better books.

Many leaders hate 'yes-men', people who constantly say yes. They hate them, because they cannot learn anything new from them.

In an interview with ABC NEWS from 1999, David Kelley, founder of IDEO (one of the world's leading innovation companies) said *"You gotta hire people who don't listen to you."*

Most people are afraid to talk to someone who doesn't agree with them. They are afraid of confrontation. They are afraid to hear 'negative' things.

But the truth is that all you will get is a different perspective. And after you get that perspective you can make the decision of whether you want to act on their ideas or not.

If you work in business, for example, I recommend you ask one of your friends who does not work in business (e.g. an artist or a doctor) about his or her ideas to problems that you're trying to solve.

The best way of course is to have friends who can fulfill that role, but if that's not an option you can also join professional groups.

Make friends with people who think differently to you.

If you are a scientist visit an arts group. If you are a designer visit an investment group. The more opposite the group is to what you're doing right now, the more different the perspective will be. Hence the more weird and different ideas you can get.

When I first moved to Canada, I didn't have many friends so I visited lots and lots of different groups and seminars.

From topics on business trade to how to become a millionaire to presentation skills to various churches to groups dedicated to health research, and so on.

I can confidently say that I met lots and lots of people who had a very different perspective on various topics.

First it was shocking to me, but now in the long run I know that it has helped me a lot in understanding and relating to various groups of people, and gave me an insight into the perspectives from which they look at problems.

In short, it has helped me come up with new ideas for business much faster.

Next time you meet new people who have a different perspective on things to you, your job is to shut up, listen, take notes and later think about how you can use their perspectives to come up with better ideas to your problems.

This is a good thing, NOT a bad thing, even though conventional wisdom will tell you differently.

(A little reminder on the side: To become truly creative and innovative you often have to go AGAINST what conventional wisdom says.)

No matter how you do it, if you want to gain a new perspective, see your problem from many different angles and gain new ideas, talk to people who disagree with you.

Who can you talk to who disagrees with you?

Great innovators enjoy people who disagree with them. They seek them out. They enjoy gaining new ideas and new perspectives.

Innovation into Action

Which people, who generally disagree with you, could you talk about your innovation problems with?

Person A: _____

Person B: _____

Group A: _____

Group B: _____

Do The Opposite (DTO)

"All progress occurs because people dare to be different."

Harry Millner

Another way to become more creative is by doing the opposite (DTO).

Doing the opposite means doing things the opposite way to how you usually do them in your daily life.

A famous example of doing the opposite is presented by Lawrence Katz and Manning Rubin in their book 'Keep Your Brain Alive: 83 Neurobics Exercises'.

They recommend readers to brush their teeth with the opposite hand.

So, if you brush your teeth with your right hand, brush them today with your left hand. This way you will create new neuron-connections in your brain and increase your creativity without any extra effort.

The other benefit is also that often, in business, to create a new product or service, you need to look at it things from an opposite perspective.

Here are a couple more ideas that have worked for me very well over the years:

- Use the remote control with your other hand

- Write or draw with your other hand

- Walk backwards when jogging or power walking

- When you are supposed to leave your shoes on, take them off

- Wear your watch on your other arm

- Sleep with your head on the other end of the bed

- Answer your cell phone on your other ear

- Use your fork and knife (or chopsticks) with your other hand

- If you usually sit on a chair, try sitting on the floor

- Put your wallet in your other pocket

- If you usually eat while sitting, try eating while standing or walking

- Do things with your eyes closed

- Try sports with your other hand (e.g. tennis, basketball, etc.)

Doing the opposite will help you quickly build new connections in your brain and you will become more creative.

My favorite benefit of the whole thing is that it takes almost no extra time, only a little bit of effort at the beginning.

Soon you will figure out that you can quickly learn to do things the opposite way. You then have the option and can choose which way you prefer doing things.

There is one famous example that shows how quickly our brain can adjust to doing the opposite:

In 1890 George Stratton invented and tested the 'upside-down glasses'. When you wore his glasses the entire world turned upside down.

Later NASA conducted tests with their astronauts using the glasses to help their astronauts adjust to disorientation in space.

NASA asked their astronauts to wear the glasses for several weeks, 24 hours a day. They asked their astronauts to function 'normally' in the upside-down condition.

Within 3-4 weeks ALL the astronauts had adjusted to the new conditions and they were able to function as normally as they did before wearing the glasses.

What that means is that within 3-4 weeks their brain had rewired their neuron-connections to help them function normally.

They were from then on able to live in both worlds: the 'normal' world and the 'upside-down' world.

As you can see, our brains allow us to adapt to the most unusual circumstances.

Our brains CAN be retrained.

Using DTO strategies, your creativity will increase and so will your ability to solve business problems (because you should now be able to see things from the opposite perspective).

Great Innovators do the opposite!

Innovation into Action

What are 5 things that you could try out DTO-style this month?

1. _____

2. _____

3. _____

4. _____

5. _____

Ask Weird Questions

"The reasonable man adapts himself to the world; the unreasonable one persists in trying to adapt the world to himself. Therefore all progress depends on the unreasonable man."

George Bernard Shaw

When Albert Einstein was 16 years old, he asked himself a weird question: 'What would it be like to ride a beam of light?'

Einstein always asked questions that seemingly no one dared to ask or considered asking. Here are a few other examples:

"What is time?"

"Is the arm on the clock moving around the room or is the room moving around the arm on the clock?"

"What powered the Big Bang?"

"What happens to space, time, and matter at the edge of a black hole?"

"What is the mysterious 'dark' energy puling the Universe apart?"

Ultimately many of his weird questions led to answers and made him one of the most famous and respected beings on the planet.

When the Wright Brothers asked themselves: "How can we fly?" it was a very weird question for most people, at that time, to ask.

Imagine how our lives would be different if the Wright brothers hadn't asked themselves how humans could fly like birds.

When Bill Gates asked himself 'How can I put a computer into every household in America?' it was also a very weird question to ask at that time (remember the size of old computers?)

The founders of Google most likely must have asked themselves "Does a search engine that analyzes the relationship between websites produce better ranking of results than current search engines do?"

Google founders Larry Page and Sergey Brin were ultimately right in their quest given that Google is the #1 search engine in the world today.

If any genius of his or her time would have asked a normal person their weird questions, they would have been considered crazy.

What 'normal' people don't understand is that asking for the impossible brings about the possible. The only way to create what most people think is impossible is to ask for it.

Every question gets an answer. That's how our brain is designed. Our brain is an answer-giving machine.

The funny thing is that when we were children we knew how to ask strange questions like "Mommy, why is the sky blue?"

Sadly what happened next was that our left brain-centered educational system kicked in and at some point we learned not to ask any more 'stupid questions'.

So, to get back to creativity and to that state of asking for the impossible, start asking yourself weird questions.

Understand that it's OK to ask them. Understand that all geniuses of all times have done so. Understand that other so-called 'normal people' will NOT understand why you ask yourself such strange and stupid things. And that's OK!

Once you learn how to ask weird questions and start getting great answers, you will fully understand Adidas's slogan "Impossible is Nothing."

When I started out as an author I often had one question on my mind: "What is the fastest way I can write a book?"

Once I asked that question, I discovered many other authors who had written their books extremely fast. One famous master writer even shares his secrets for writing a book in 14 days in an ebook he sells at www.writeabooknow.com.

I started learning how "fast authors" think and then developed my own way of doing it.

Even though I'm not always 100% successful, 2 of the 4 books I have written, were done in about 2 weeks without editing.

Later in this book, you will get a list of the questions you can ask yourself to create almost any product or service you desire much faster compared to the average person (and in many cases even your average so-called expert).

The weirder the question, the weirder the answer. And often the weirder the answer, the more innovative the results.

Great innovators ask weird questions!

Innovation into Action

What weird question can you constantly ask yourself that would automatically lead to an innovation in your industry if you could find an answer to it?

_____

_____

Basic 2

InnoTeam

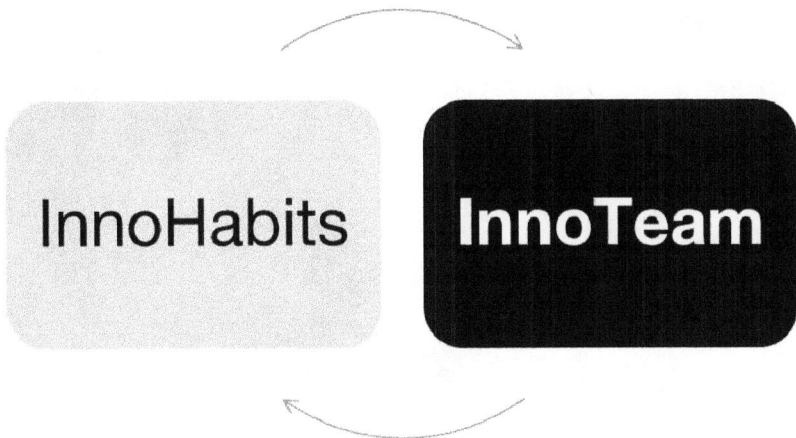

Why InnoTeam?!

The Problem in a Nutshell

Most people try to create innovations by themselves (also called the "lone wolf syndrome"). Ultimately almost all of them fail miserably. Why is that?

And then there are teams whose sole purpose is to create innovations, yet only have average or low output, even though they spend a lot of time working on their ideas. Why is that?

The Purpose of InnoTeam

The purpose of InnoTeam is to help you become aware of the importance of creating the RIGHT team for innovation to take place, as well as to discover what others' (not to mention your own) innovation strengths and weaknesses are.

This part of the book will tackle both of these issues.

You will learn about the 11 InnoTypes, the eleven different innovation personality types that are needed to create great innovations.

People who consider themselves "lone wolves" will learn how to build and work with a team without needing to change their work style too much.

Ultimately, you will be able to create a great team, not based on guess work, but based on individuals' strengths, which you will be able to more easily identify.

Use this section when you either want to BUILD or EXPAND your team.

Get ready to build your InnoTeam!

The 'Perfect' Innovator

We all know stories of winners in life; people who achieve success all by themselves through lots of sweat and personal effort. Often they are called "self-made".

When it comes to innovation the same thing seems to be true. We believe that there are 'perfect innovators', who run around overflowing with ideas and execute those ideas all by themselves.

Bill Gates is the innovator of Windows; Steve Jobs is the innovator of the iPod, and Colonel Sanders is the innovator of the KFC chicken recipe. If you think about it you can probably come up with dozens more success stories.

In Western cultures we tend to reward the individual.

Our movies show how one person saves the planet, how one superhero stops the villain, and how one person discovers the Promised Land.

We tend to think that it is one person who wins in business, in war, and even in innovation.

Yet it is this kind of thinking that is not only false, but in terms of innovating new products or services, can even be extremely misleading.

No one ever becomes successful alone!

There is not such thing as the 'Perfect Innovator'.

Innovation success is achieved through the collaboration of a handful (and often more) of people who are all extremely good at what they do, but who more often than not, have completely different points of views and expertise.

To make an idea successful, you need a team of people with diverse backgrounds and expertise. What matters most is this variety of input.

Another common misconception relates to what the 'perfect innovator' looks like.

Often, we imagine the advertising-look-a-like, super-fashionable, tech-savvy, yet suave uber-human.

Of course this is just an image, and nothing more.

In reality innovators come in all shapes and sizes, like everything else in life.

Some innovators look a mess, some are really well-dressed. Some innovators have the latest gadgets, some innovators hate the latest gadgets. Some innovators are geeks, some are not.

The only thing that all innovators have in common, are the principles described in this book.

Innovators come in all shapes and sizes.

As a matter of fact, often the reason they are so innovative is that they are completely different from most people.

So, don't worry too much about your style. All innovators have their own, unique style.

Just make sure you get the right team together when you're innovating. In this chapter I will show you the personality types you'll need to have on your team.

Innovation into Action

What are some your beliefs about the 'perfect innovator' and why do you think they are NOT necessarily the true about real innovators?

_____

_____

_____

Innovation Teams

"So when a good idea comes, you know, part of my job is to move it around, just see what different people think, get people talking about it, argue with people about it, get ideas moving among that group of 100 people, get different people together to explore different aspects of it quietly, and, you know - just explore things."

Steve Jobs, Apple Inc. CEO

What's better for coming up with creative ideas: using 1 brain or 100?

Most people would say 100. Some people would say 'That depends on the brains'. Few people would say 1.

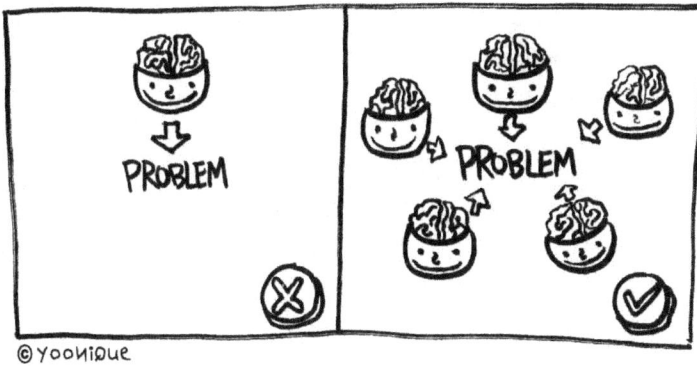

© yoonique

As I've mentioned before, to get great ideas you need to think outside of the box and get as many different approaches and points of views as possible.

Innovating with a team will help you do just that.

Often the more different the people involved, the better.

The biggest problem of course is what inevitably happens when multiple brains come together (especially the ones with totally different points of view): CHAOS and DISCORD!

Chaos and discord are to be expected in a situation where your team tries to innovate.

The key of course is not to fear it, but understand that it's just part of the process. You should actually enjoy it. Even though it's tough, ultimately it's good!

To make sure that people don't kill each other though, it's good to understand the innovation process a little bit more and we will talk about that later in this book.

Working together with a team to come up with new ideas might seem difficult at first, but you will usually also come up with the best ideas.

Having said that, please note that some innovators act like lone wolves. Even though most people work better in teams, some just don't. Some people actually come up with better ideas working alone.

If you think you are a lone wolf, my strong suggestion to you is to create an innovation team that you meet every now and then to pick their brains or to outsource certain tasks to them.

Even lone wolves need a team to innovate.

Even though lone wolves come up with a lot of great ideas on their own, they can improve their results by meeting with specific people who have different points of view and can help them see what they cannot see (no one is perfect after all).

ABC TV once filmed IDEO - one of the world's leading design and innovation consulting companies. In the program, they challenged the team to innovate on a new product within one week.

The team consisted of a colorful mix of people from various backgrounds: 1 engineer, 1 MBA graduate, 1 linguist, 1 marketing expert, 1 psychologist, and 1 biology major.

Could the team have been more diverse?

What IDEO, like all innovative companies, understands is that team members with diverse backgrounds lead to teams that generate diverse ideas.

Great innovators work with great teams. That way they innovate faster and easier.

Innovation into Action

Who is on your team right now? And what do you think their strengths and weaknesses with regards to innovation might be? Writing down their names, strengths and weaknesses will help you identify what other members you might need on your team:

Name	Strength	Weakness
_____	_____	_____
_____	_____	_____
_____	_____	_____
_____	_____	_____

The 11 InnoTypes

"Different strokes for different folks." Proverb

What's your Innovation Type? Chances are you don't know! Most people don't.

I, for one, didn't have a class called 'Innovation Personalities 101' when I went to school. Maybe you can relate…

In the following section, I will share with you 'The 11 InnoTypes'. The 11 InnoTypes describe eleven innovation personalities: their strengths and their weaknesses.

Being a trainer and consultant I've over the years learned a lot about personality tests like Enneagram, MBTI (Myers-Briggs Type Indicator), DISC (Dominant, Influence, Steadiness, Conscientiousness), and so on.

Also, I've tried to find out as much as I could about 'innovation personalities'. The one source I found quite useful was from IDEO's General Manager Tom Kelly who wrote the book 'The 10 Faces of Innovation', describing ten different innovation personalities.

The 11 InnoTypes are different though.

When I created (or better said discovered) the 11 InnoTypes I started off going back through all the products or services I've created over the years, all the products my clients had created and all the interviews I'd had with successful entrepreneurs and innovators and how they'd created their products and services.

Also, I took the approach of the ENTREPRENEUR (or intrapreneur) when creating the 11 InnoTypes.

As I mentioned earlier, to be a true innovator you need to come from an entrepreneurial or intrapreneurial perspective.

Many tasks can be delegated, but ultimately you need to be the one who gets things rolling by finding the right people for your team.

You will find the 11 InnoTypes to be very simple. Simple is good. Simple means you can easily identify the types in your day-to-day life and find the right people fast. In my opinion this is one of the major drawbacks of many personality tests: you simply cannot get everyone you meet to take an online personality test before you can work with them.

When reading through this section, I want you to focus on the following two things:

1. Discover which type(s) best describes you.

2. Discover which types you are missing in yourself and on your team. Then I want you to 'fill' the unfilled spots.

The reason for this is that each of the 11 InnoTypes is necessary to create a killer innovation. If one is lacking often that is the missing piece of an innovation's success.

Here's a quick overview of the "11 InnoTypes":

InnoType1: The Starter

InnoType2: The Strategist

InnoType3: The Researcher

InnoType4: The Geek

InnoType5: The Connector

InnoType6: The Creator

InnoType7: The Fool

InnoType8: The Destroyer

InnoType9: The Designer

InnoType10: The Marketer

InnoType11: The Bulldog

Caution!

The InnoTypes are NOT mutually exclusive. Many people have within themselves at least 2 or more of the InnoTypes (with their respective strengths and weaknesses).

So, if you find you have more than one, be happy. What that means is that you most likely have to find fewer people for your team. Plus you will be able to understand more of the people on your team. It's truly a benefit.

InnoType1: **The Starter**

The first InnoType is the Starter. The Starter is the first person needed on any team. The reason Starters are so important is that without them no innovation project can take off. They are the entrepreneurs of the innovation world and necessary to get things moving.

The Starter's biggest strength is to get the whole team started. They are often the ones who get everyone together and also the ones who create the initial vision/challenge for the project.

What often happens is that a Starter is having a conversation with someone or walking down the street or taking a shower and 'Boom!' out of nowhere a great idea pops into their heads.

Usually this idea is just a rough concept (don't expect Starters to provide details, that's not their strength), but after that Starters get the right people together, get them excited about the idea and (of course) get them started.

Another strength of theirs is that they can easily get others to take the right action, and to act on it quickly.

The Starter's weakness in an innovation team is that they usually want to start too many different ideas at the same time. Also, they are great at starting, but not so good at completing projects.

InnoType2: **The Strategist**

The second InnoType is the Strategist. Strategists are great at planning projects, giving them structure and coming up with the overall strategies. They are true masters at turning ideas into measurable, specific action plans.

Also, Strategists are often good at finding solutions to problems that come up along the way and knowing who can best solve them.

Another strength Strategists have is that they can keep the big picture alive while everyone is pushing forward to make the vision a reality.

Strategists are the central point of the innovation process hence they are the ones everyone will talk to (often in combination with Starters) whenever problems arise. They understand every role well enough to fully support them.

Another ability Strategists have is to get everyone back on track if they lose focus, which usually happens in the often chaotic creative process. Part of this is also that they make sure that projects get completed.

Their weakness is that sometimes they tend to over-plan and over-strategize everything before actually taking action.

Make sure you connect Strategists with people who can apply their plans and turn them into reality fast.

InnoType3: **The Researcher**

The third Innotype is the Researcher. Researchers are good at finding stacks of information. Researchers are excellent at researching online and with written material (books, magazines, newspapers, etc.) to add valuable ideas. Researchers love data, details and any special ideas and information that they can share.

It's easy to spot a researcher based on one or several of the following:

Books – they know a huge variety not just on one topic, but on all topics from history to self-help to novels.

Websites – they know a huge variety of websites, all having a benefit for something.

Magazines/Newspapers – they read everything they can get their hands on from Scientific American to People to US Weekly to The New York Times to Vogue.

TV Shows – they tend to watch anything and everything, They are master zippers who will watch anything as long as it's entertaining and worthy of being shared with others.

Without researchers your team will lack the valuable information and data you need to support your ideas. Also in terms of quantity of ideas, without a researcher, you will be left behind. Usually only one in one hundred ideas has real value for a project, so quantity is really a key success factor.

Researchers are very much detail-oriented. They can find information faster than anyone. They know where to search and how to search fast. They are often happy to be the first to find an idea, and love TV shows like Jeopardy where they can prove their general knowledge.

Use them especially in early innovation stages where it's really all about the quantity of information.

Their weakness is that they don't know what to do with all the data and information that they've found. They lack the skill to turn their information into a product or service.

Also, they tend to overwhelm others with their information. They tend to simply share too much. Ask them to edit their information beforehand and share only their most important findings.

InnoType4: **The Geek**

The fourth InnoType is the Geek. The Geek is the expert on the team; the person who knows more than everybody else about the product or service and its industry.

Geeks are extreme experts in one specific topic where their knowledge is very in-depth (topics can range from anything from IT to horses to cars to collecting stamps).

Geeks can often be identified just based on how they are dressed, how their office or home is arranged or by the people they hang out with (usually people just like themselves).

Without a Geek on your team you will lack in-depth experience and knowledge about the industry for which you want to create your innovation.

The Geek's strength is that they can give you in-depth information that would take you 10 years of studying their field to comprehend, let alone recall from memory.

Also, they are extremely passionate about their chosen field and believe it is the most important thing in the world (yes, even stamp collectors, who will tell you the historical importance of stamps and how they survived through the centuries, and why stamp collecting is not appreciated enough).

Geeks can give you a huge advantage over the competition.

Their biggest weakness is probably their terminology. To put it in simple terms: no one understands what they're saying.

Think of the computer Geek who spits out terms and abbreviations you don't understand (unless you are one yourself). This was precisely the problem I faced, when I started working with employees of Microsoft.

And because they use such advanced terminology, they often have a hard time connecting and communicating effectively with others.

Think of movies like Independence Day where a Geek is trying to tell the President that the world will go under if he doesn't act now, but fails to be convincing at first because no-one can comprehend the message.

And because others don't fully understand them, Geeks can easily get annoyed with other people outside their circle of Geeks.

To overcome this problem, you need a "translator" or a geek open-minded enough to explain their thoughts in plain language to the other members of the team.

InnoType5: **The Connector**

The fifth InnoType is the Connector. The Connector is the master of relationships. Connectors know half the city, or in some cases half the world (at least that's what they'd like you to believe).

Connectors gain valuable information from meeting others. They're able to join a new meeting they've neither attended before nor have a clue about, and walk out having half the room not only liking them, but sharing choice information with them too.

They are also really good at bringing onboard key people such as investors or marketing channels, without breaking a sweat.

Without a Connector you might not get enough input from many different types of people. Connectors might not always find the perfect clients, but they can get ideas from various people which often leads to unique ideas.

The Connector's weakness can be that they are far too people-focused. They need to be around people and constantly be in motion. They often have a hard time sitting still and prefer spending 100% of their time outside meeting people instead of inside sitting behind a desk.

This strength can sometimes be a weakness when they spend too much time with the team, because Connectors like to talk.

And when they are with the team for too long, they will frequently interrupt them with trivial things just to keep the conversation going.

Make sure that you send your Connectors out into the field to meet new people who can contribute to the project.

InnoType6: **The Creator**

The sixth InnoType is the Creator. The Creator is the one on the team who actually creates the product or service. Creators love creating, testing and solving problems related to product or service-development.

They are the ones who know all the rules, the right timing, the principles and the standards of creating the product or service.

A Creator will hear an idea or a concept and already be half-way done with the creation in her own mind.

Creators create prototypes quickly, ask for feedback, test, test, test, and keep solving problems and mistakes until they're finally resolved.

Their big weakness is that they tend to fall in love with their product while forgetting that the real thing to be falling in love with is the end user.

You can probably think of a couple of people right now who fell so much in love with their products, but ended up not selling much of it, because not many others felt the same.

To prevent this from happening make sure that they fully engage with the Marketer to understand who they are creating the product for.

Creators can create amazing products, but only if they are reminded of the people who end up using the product. If not, they might shoot in the wrong direction.

InnoType7: **The Fool**

The seventh InnoType is the Fool. Fools are probably the easiest type to understand, yet often the hardest to find.

The Fool's biggest strength is that they take a product or test a service, and by sheer chance find a huge problem that no one else has spotted.

For example, if you create a new phone and are certain it is indestructible, give it to a Fool to make sure that it REALLY is. If it isn't, the Fool will find the problem in less than 5 minutes.

Fools are often very clumsy, gullible and naïve. Yet at the same time they are action-takers and try out anything new that they can get their hands on.

The value they bring to the innovation table is very simple: they will break anything that can possibly be broken and make every mistake that can possibly be made.

If a true Fool tests your product or service and you fix the mistakes she makes, your product or service is truly indestructible and you can move on to mass production.

Their weakness? In case of product innovation, make sure not to give them the only prototype that you have. Because chances are, they will destroy it and you'll have to create it again from scratch.

Also, because no one likes to show that s/he is a Fool, a true Fool can sometimes be hard to find as they often have to suppress their 'talent' as much as possible around others.

InnoType8: **The Destroyer**

The eighth InnoType is the Destroyer. The Destroyer is the anti-creator.

The Destroyer is in charge of actually finding all reasons why an idea or product or service will not work. All the problems that might come up. All the barriers that might be blocking the successful creation and implementation of the innovation.

Yet compared to the Fool, the Destroyer doesn't find mistakes by chance, but by exact science.

Destroyers will go into a movie, or a shop, or to a new country, or try a new product and find a hundred problems that need fixing.

Even in situations or with products that most people would consider perfect, Destroyers will find multiple things that are not good enough, and need improving.

Their biggest strength is that they will see almost all mistakes at a glance much faster than you can imagine. Hence they will save you time and money because you can get the Creator to fix the problems they find.

Without a Destroyer you will most likely run into problems later that could have been avoided earlier. Let Destroyers show you the problems, let the rest of the team solve them.

Their one big weakness is that they tend to criticize and complain too much.

A true Destroyer might be running around your office, looking at the progress you've made and still complain that things aren't going fast enough and certain problems aren't fixed yet, so they end up upsetting and de-motivating everybody else.

The best thing you can with a Destroyer is give them a specific time when they can point out all the mistakes they've found.

This can be sometimes hard for Destroyers, because many Destroyers want to share mistakes they've found immediately, but they will appreciate being able to share their whole laundry list to an attentive (perhaps even captive) audience.

InnoType9: **The Designer**

The ninth InnoType is the Designer. The Designer is the beauty freak on the team. Designers make our world a more beautiful place. Designers make anything and everything more attractive, including your next innovation.

Without a Designer your product or service will not be half as attractive as it could be. And often in business, as with love, the more attractive product wins out over the competition.

Their biggest strength is that they take an average product or service and 'spice it up' so much that everyone who sees it falls in love with it.

Designers are responsible for the beautiful colors and the sleek shapes that we enjoy every day in great products, such as the Mini Cooper, the iPhone, Bang & Olufsen stereo systems, even whole city designs as made for Seoul, South Korea.

Designers will make sure that your product or service (or even city) really stands out looks-wise.

Designers make sure that a reality TV show looks more interesting and exciting, that a cell phone has a cool look and feel to it, and that a restaurant will have that cozy, home-away-from-home feel from first impressions to last, using feng shui and interior design principles.

The Designer's big weakness is that they often tend to spend too much time finalizing the 'perfect design'.

I remember the story of a French artist whose painting had been placed in the Louvre. A week later he was carried out by security for painting over his painting screaming "It's not done yet!" to which the security responded "If it's in the Louvre it must be finished."

Make sure that you give Designers specific deadlines in which to finish their designs.

InnoType10: **The Marketer**

The tenth InnoType is the Marketer. The Marketer is the one with the strong client orientation. Marketers always think in practical terms. They think "What's the benefit for the end user?" Marketers ensure that your product is actually desirable and sellable.

Without a Marketer chances are high that you'll create a product that the end user doesn't actually want to buy. Marketers make sure that your innovation is user-friendly and hence easy to market and sell.

Marketers are masters at finding the right target market for a product or service, or are even able to create multiple target segments for a product.

Marketers also understand fully WHY people actually buy. They understand people's motivations.

Where Creators talk about the specifications of the product, Marketers will tell you how much better you will feel and what benefits you will enjoy in your life if you choose this product.

Marketers' weakness is that they need to watch out not to over-market the product or service. Marketers live in a world focused on 'showing' value to the end user.

And sometimes they 'show' value where there is none to be found (e.g. cigarette companies), and this can sometimes lead to deceiving the client.

Make sure to make your Marketers understand that you want them to make the product or service look better, sound better and feel better than it is, but that you also want to stick to the truth and create marketing messages and packages with integrity.

InnoType11: **The Bulldog**

Last, but not least, is the Bulldog. The Bulldog is the born salesperson. Bulldogs are able to sell ice to Eskimos and still keep everyone happy.

The Bulldog's greatest strength is that they constantly sell to and meet clients. They often understand their clients' problems and dissatisfaction with a product or service very well.

Also, Bulldogs know how to 'close' a deal, i.e. how to get a client to make the final buying decision and what is needed to do so.

Bulldogs can be great testers for your 'new' product or service in front of a client. Introducing something and getting feedback is fairly simple for them.

Your innovation team can benefit from their real world experience as to why people do or don't buy your product. Then the rest of the team can find solutions to the problems that arise.

Their weakness can be that they can sometimes be too pushy with clients.

We've all experienced being pushed by a bulldog into buying a product, and then coming home to find that the product wasn't nearly as good as promised. You probably never went to their store or bought their product again because you felt cheated.

Make sure that Bulldogs understand that you want to create value for your clients, not just sell your product for the sake of making a sale.

Innovation into Action

Determine YOUR InnoTypes:

_____

_____

_____

Which InnoTypes are already on your team? Write their names and their InnoTypes down here:

_____

_____

_____

_____

Which InnoTypes are missing from your team? How could you meet them? Do you already know the right person? Write down who is missing and how (or where) you think you can find them here:

_____

_____

_____

_____

Part 2

The **4 Steps** of
Innovation

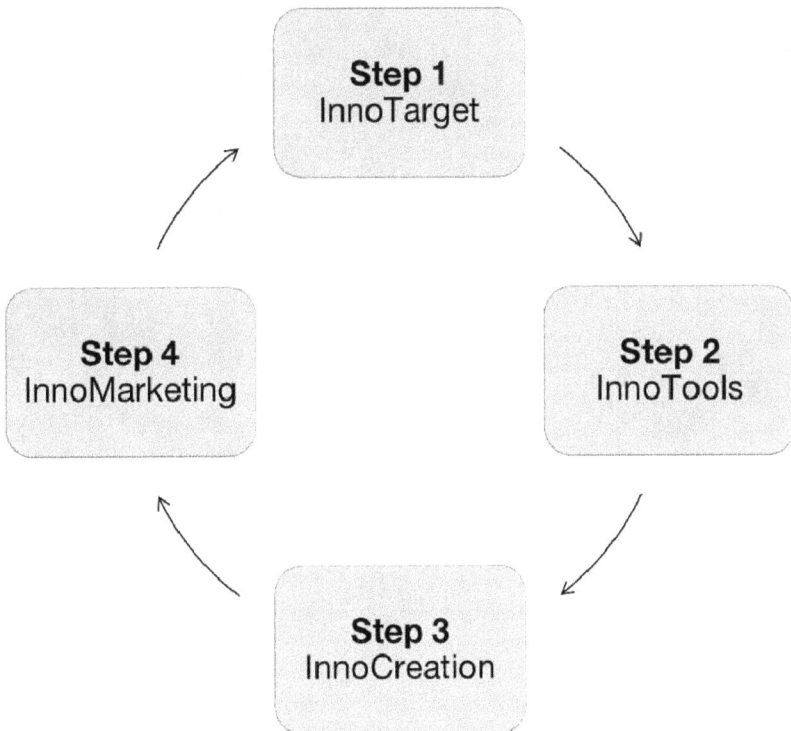

Step 1
InnoTarget

Step 2
InnoTools

Step 3
InnoCreation

Step 4
InnoMarketing

The 4 Steps of Innovation

In this section you will be introduced to the 4 Steps of Innovation, a simple 4-step process that will allow you to create innovative products or services much faster, with less effort and hopefully with a higher success rate too.

Step 1: InnoTarget will help you define what target problem you need to aim for when creating your next product or service.

Step 2: InnoTools will give you multiple brainstorming tools to solve the problem you've identified in step 1.

Steps 3: InnoCreation will show you how to turn the ideas you've come up with in step 2 into a tangible product or service.

Step 4: InnoMarketing will give you the basic strategies to better market the creation you've conceived in step 3 to the market place.

Get ready to innovate!

Step 1

InnoTarget

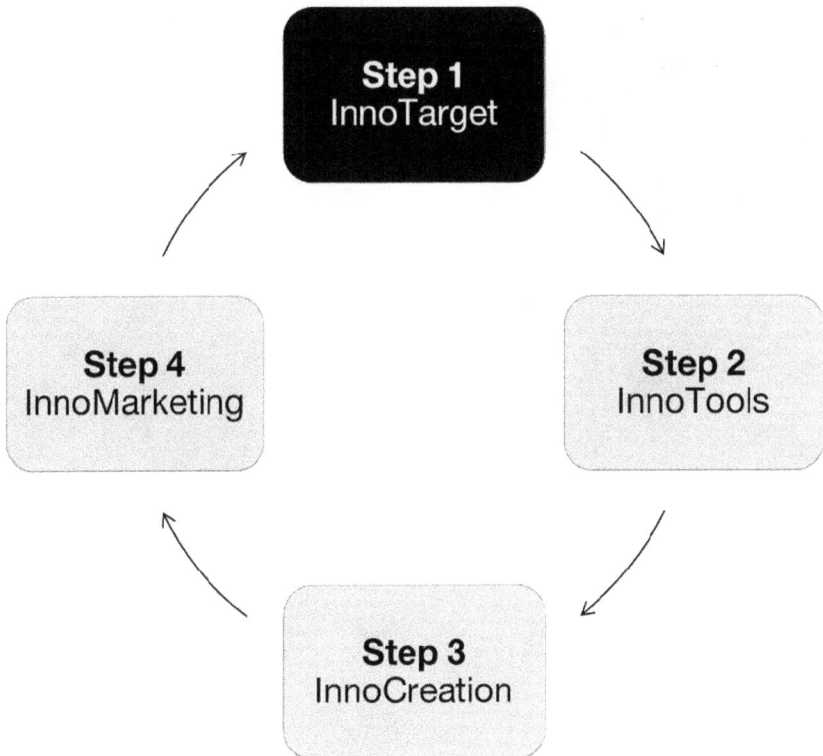

Step 1
InnoTarget

Step 4
InnoMarketing

Step 2
InnoTools

Step 3
InnoCreation

Why **Step 1:** InnoTarget?!

The Problem in a Nutshell

Most ideas are doomed from the start.

It's often NOT the creativity, NOT the team, NOT the spark that matters, but the START of the innovative process.

What do people aim for? Most teams start with the WRONG TARGETS.

They start innovating with things relating to their product or service that THEY think should be improved on.

And hence (often) all their efforts from this stage onward will be doomed unless they go back to this initial stage to reassess what they're doing.

The Purpose of InnoTarget

> The purpose of InnoTarget is to hammer into your brain the TARGET to aim for whenever you want to create an innovation: Your ideal users and THEIR problems and unmet needs.

In this part of the book you will learn why most inventions fail (no matter how much money companies invest in marketing), and MOST IMPORTANTLY how to determine your ideal user and their problems.

Using what you learn in the following pages will give you the cutting edge over the competition, because you will learn how to do what they don't do. You will also learn what is also defined by the world's leading innovators as the no. 1 step to creating innovations.

When to Use InnoTarget

WHENEVER you are out to create a new product or service that you want to see succeed in the market place.

The art lies in the start, and the chances of reaping rewards will increase tenfold.

Get ready to determine your InnoTarget!

Failed Inventions

"[The APPLE Lisa] was a great machine. We just couldn't sell any."

Bruce Tognazzini, APPLE Employee #66

Every year millions of new products and services are created. The sad thing is just that…

…most of them fail!

How many people do you know who have something they've created lying in their basement?

Off the top of my head, I can instantly think of several people I've met in my life (some of them my friends) who have created something that ended up collecting dust in their basements.

I too have created several products that have failed (from a CD program that no one wanted to a "new" planner that didn't fit into anyone's bag).

The funny (and sad) thing is that many of these wannabe innovators did actually come up with some pretty good ideas.

And if you listen to them talk about their products for long enough, they might even persuade you that the product is great.

So why is it that most of these creations have ended up in the basement? (or an old shoebox, or in the corner of a closet, or whichever other sad place they've been relegated to).

Why do most products in the marketplace fail?

Why do even products created by big companies fail?

97

Here are some of the world's most famous products that failed:

- Ford Edsel
- The New Coke
- Crystal Pepsi
- Life Savers Soda
- Apple's Lisa Computer
- IBM's PC Junior
- Sony Betamax
- Cosmopolitan Yogurt
- Microsoft Web TV
- Coors Rocky Mountain Spring Water
- Cocaine Energy Drink
- Earring Magic Ken
- Colgate Kitchen Entrees
- Apple Newton
- DeLorean Car
- Kellogg's Breakfast Mates
- Bottled Water for Pets
- Bic Underwear
- Harley Davidson Perfume
- Levi's Shoes
- RJ Reynolds' Smokeless Cigarettes
- BenGay Aspirin
- Webvan
- Levi's Type 1 Jeans
- Nintendo Virtual Boy

All of these products failed. The companies that developed them spent millions of dollars creating them and marketing them, and yet they failed anyway.

So, how high are your chances of winning in the game of innovation in business if you don't have the abundant resources that these companies did?

The good news is that you actually do stand a pretty good chance of succeeding.

The success of an innovation has little to do with money invested (even though you will need money to finance whatever it is you create). Also, often you don't need a big brand name behind you to create a great innovation (though of course it wouldn't hurt either).

The reasons why inventions fail to catch on (and by extension to become innovations) are quite different to what you'd expect.

Innovation into Action

What failed inventions can you think of and why did they fail?

Invention   Why it failed

————   ——————————————————

————   ——————————————————

————   ——————————————————

————   ——————————————————

————   ——————————————————

Why Most Inventions Fail!

"Failure is not falling down but refusing to get up."

Chinese Proverb

Why do most inventions fail to become innovations?

What are the secret reasons that most creators, companies and most of the general public don't understand?

An invention fails to become an innovation for one or more of the following five reasons:

1. "We don't know our end user."

This is the most basic mistake that innovators make.

Companies create products or services without their end user in mind.

If you don't know who the end user of your product or service will be, it is hard to predict if the product or service will be a success or not.

So many inventions are created not because they fulfill a need or a problem experienced by a group of end users, but because the inventor (or the company the inventor works for) thinks it's a great idea.

Marketing's most basic lesson: Don't start marketing (or creating your product in this case) without first knowing who your target is and what they want and need.

Who is Coors Beer's target market? Beer drinkers.

Do beer drinkers care much about their health? Not really.

Are beer drinkers interested in drinking fresh "Rocky Mountain Spring Water" created by their favorite beer brand? Most likely not.

Would water drinkers be interested in buying water from a beer company? Probably not.

Coors has done terrifically in the beer market, but not so well with their water because they forgot their end users and their needs and wants.

Almost all of the services or products I've created that have done just average or that failed were usually related to my own failure to study my ideal end user.

I thought I had the greatest idea which just felt "right" and so I just went straight to production without giving any thought to my end users. From my experience that is almost always a bad move, yet so many creators from FORTUNE 500 company staff to small business owners make it too often and wonder why their product or service has failed.

> **Most innovations fail as a result of little or no understanding of the target user and her needs.**

2. "We don't know our competitors."

I do not believe in copying or benchmarking competitors, but I do believe in competitor research for the sake of finding innovation niches.

You'll want to know what your competitors are doing for three reasons:

a. to figure out what they do poorly and see if you can create an innovation that solves the problems they may be creating.

b. to check if they are overlooking a target user group in the market.

c. to see if an industry standard is coming up that you need to align yourself to (or find yourself out of business).

Remember Sony Betamax? Chances are you don't.

During its release Sony Betamax was superior to VHS, which came out at about the same time. It had better sound, better picture quality, and even a better price.

Yet it failed in the market place.

Why?

Because ALL of Sony's competitors decided to go with VHS. And if the rest of the world is against you, you have to follow or else you're left fighting for your life.

Sony Betamax failed because Sony didn't read the global trend of its competitors (or pushed them to follow theirs).

3. "We don't know what the latest trends are."

On my desk next to me is my old, beloved Samsung Q30 notebook. Released in 2005 and one of the first mini computers in the world, it prided itself on being flat. It was only available here in South Korea.

102

I bought it for about 2,500,000 Korean Won (about 1,800 Euros) at the time. I saw it online in Germany for 3,990 Euros.

Today, in 2009, I can find a similar notebook for about 700,000 Korean Won. Similar look. Flat and light as well. Better functions. More power.

Why is it that I can buy a new computer for about 1/3 of the price of my old one? And a far better performing one at that.

One of the reasons, of course, you will say is that the world keeps turning and computers are getting cheaper.

That's true. But I'm talking in this case about one of the world's first mini computers.

The trend that started in about late 2007 is that more and more people the world over have started using mini computers.

A trend was created. Prices started dropping thanks to a Taiwanese company called ASUS that focused on producing only mini computers, and for cheap.

Soon everyone followed ASUS: HP, Samsung, LG, SONY, virtually all the big players in the industry.

Why? Because that was where the market was going - small, affordable notebooks.

Watch out for trends!

4. "We don't know how to create a product or service that's simple and sexy."

If your product or service has some serious birth defects no marketing in the world can help it.

Many products and services simply aren't good enough.

So you may have chosen the right target market, you may have found a niche that your competitors have overlooked, and even kept your ears to the ground to keep abreast of the latest trends.

But if your product or service isn't superior, simple and sexy, chances are that it will NOT succeed.

Microsoft' Vista operating system is a great example. Perfect target market (almost anyone using a PC). It followed the prevailing trends with its increased functionality and sleeker design. And yet everyone hated it.

Many people I know who have used it preferred to rollback to an older version of Windows. Maybe you have too.

Vista has received lots of criticism regarding its hardware requirements, restrictive licensing terms, digital rights management restrictions, and so on. In 2009 after having been released for just under 2 years it still had far less market share of worldwide operating systems compared to the older version Windows XP. Vista had an 18.6% market share, while the "outdated" XP had 63.3% market share.

In the end it Vista may have looked a bit sexier than its predecessor, but it certainly wasn't simpler to use.

Remember this when you create your next product or service, else you'll end up with your end users talking about your product - just not in a good way.

5. "We don't know how to market our product or service."

Many products and services simply fail because of poor marketing.

This is probably the worst mistake of all.

What if you had a great product or service and no one knew about it?

For example, the first versions of a working "internet" were developed in the 70s and used since 1975 by the Department of Defense of the US army. But it wasn't until the late 80s that it received public interest. What if the internet's benefits would have been more clear to the world 10 or 15 years earlier? How different would our world look today?

Many great products never see the light of day, because of poor packaging, poor choice of marketing channels, poor description, poor presentation, poor PR, or simply because they weren't marketed enough.

This can also be true for the marketing of a whole country.

South Korea is probably one of the most under-marketed countries on the planet.

It's country number 12 or 13 in terms of GDP, and one of the richest countries on the planet. Its capital Seoul is a very exciting, 24-hour, non-stop, energetic city that easily compares with New York, London or Tokyo. The possibilities for leisure are endless from the best mountains for skiing and hiking to world class beaches, Korea has it all.

Korean actors and singers renowned all over Asia. From drama TV shows to music to movies, to the point that authorities in countries like China, Japan, Thailand and Malaysia fear that Korean pop culture is becoming way too popular.

And yet…we in the west hardly know anything about South Korea.

Unfortunately not only is the country's marketing not yet strong enough, but it receives lots of bad marketing due to its volatile neighbor: North Korea.

When I first moved here more than 5 years ago, I couldn't believe my eyes. What a great place! And yet, in advance I knew nothing about it. Now I tell everyone about how great it is.

I'm confident that in the future South Korea will definitely do better regarding its marketing, but at least for now it is under-marketed and definitely 'Asia's best kept secret' to the west.

Great innovators not only create, but also properly market their products and services.

Ideal Users

Who is the ideal user for your products or services?

Your ideal users (and their problems/unmet needs) is your InnoTarget!

Understanding who your ideal users are and what their problems and unmet needs are is the biggest key to creating incredible innovations.

Whenever you start innovating you need to InnoTarget your users and the problems and unmet needs that they face.

To get a clear InnoTarget, you need to REALLY understand your target user (we'll talk about problems and unmet needs in the next chapter).

The more you figure out who your ideal user is and what they want, the easier it will be for you to create something that they are interested in.

There are two main ways to determine your ideal user: demographics and psychographics.

| **Demographics** |
| Age |
| Job position |
| Marital status |
| Income level |
| Area they live in |
| Education |

Demographics are things like age, job position, marital status, income level, area they live in, education, etc.

| **Psychographics** |
| Magazines |
| TV Shows |
| Places travelled |
| Clothing Style |
| Type of Car |
| Type of Friends |

For example, creating a car for a 50-year old male with a wife and 3 kids versus creating a car for an 18-year male will be two very different endeavors.

Psychographics are about the lifestyle of your ideal users, how they think and what their values are.

This includes the magazines they read, TV shows they watch, places they travel to, what type of clothes they buy. It's all based on what's going on inside their heads and what their lifestyles looks like based on that.

For example, the cellular phone you create for the adventurous traveler type would be quite different to the one you create for the conservative accountant.

Putting it simply - by determining demographics you find out *who* your target users are, by determining psychographics you find out *why* they are your target users.

To create an innovative product or service you need to first understand WHO your users are and WHY they would want to buy your product or service, BEFORE you start creating it.

Most inventors do the opposite.

Most product or service creators start creating their product or service first, and then go looking for their final target users.

[P.S. The worst target user you can possibly choose is "everyone" unless of course you create an elixir of eternal youth, and even that probably wouldn't be to everyone's taste.]

Let me give you an example of why being unclear about your target user almost always leads to failure.

A QUICK STORY

Imagine it is 1997 and you want to create a website where people can communicate and get to know each other better.

You have $50,000 savings you want to invest in this business.

So, you start creating a website you think is terrific. Great design. Great features. Very user-friendly. You've invested your money and time to create it and you've done a great job.

But you now have a problem.

You have to make money.

So, what do you do?

You put a price tag on your careful created website.

You let people sign up under the condition that they have a "test month" to test out your website and then you make them pay on a monthly basis.

Let's say you think big, so you set a target of signing up 100,000 (the internet is huge after all). Next you want to become rich, so what price tag do you put on monthly user rate? $15!

Next you calculate your quick way to riches: 100,000 x $15 = $1,500,000 per month. That's $18,000,000 in sales per year.

Minus expenses, you calculate, you walk away with a nice $10,000,000, maybe more, in your pocket EVERY YEAR.

Not bad, you think.

Happy about your plan you upload the website and start marketing.

Being clear about your future goal you invest more of your money in online advertising and online pop-ups (because that's the sure-fire way to get more clients nowadays) and wait.

You sit in front of your computer checking the sign up rate.

People are coming.

Oh YEAH!

The first day it's 12 users...

...then 27...

...then 49...

...and so on. By the end of the month you've signed up 956 users with your smart marketing and witty sales copy on the welcome page.

Then the first day of the next month's hits.

You wake up. You are excited. How many users have signed up as paid members???

(Last night you did a quick calculation on how much money you can make just in the first month if have half the users signed up: around $5,000!!!)

You jump to your computer.

You turn it on.

How many? How many???

You see the number.

Your jaw drops...

...

Only 3 people paid!

You can't believe it.

What went wrong???

In wonder you ask yourself: "What's wrong with THEM? Didn't they see the VALUE?"

After some thinking, you conclude that something must be wrong with THEM. That THEY didn't see the value and are the WRONG group. Using positive thinking you continue your plan, because it must be 'right'.

You continue your plan for another 4 months.

…

After 4 months, you are broke.

You've spent all of your money and have only 11 subscribers. On top of that, a few of the 11 users you do have keep sending you complaint emails that there are not enough others and that if you cannot bring in more members, they will also cancel their membership.

Frustrated you close the business, thinking 'no one saw my vision'…

WHAT IS WRONG ABOUT THE ABOVE STORY?

There are several things. But at the core it is very simple: This innovator/entrepreneur didn't think hard enough about her target users.

What was the main characteristic of people in 1997 using the internet?

THEY DIDN'T WANT TO PAY.

Even today, people don't want to pay for stuff online.

This innovator/entrepreneur only thought of payment from users as a revenue stream, whereas she could have thought of website advertisements instead to achieve her revenue goal.

If she would have studied her target users a little more closely, she could have easily figured out that they didn't want to spend their money online and then would have been forced to come up with a new revenue strategy for her business.

I'm taking this example of the internet here, because understanding and serving most internet users has been one of the greatest marketing shifts in our world: offer a service for free, yet find another way to make money.

Nowadays there are membership websites making money mainly through advertisements or having different user status levels, so even if users don't pay from the start they can use the website for an unlimited amount of time, but with limited user functions because they haven't paid.

The other point is that, if our entrepreneur above focused the business more on a certain target group, e.g. university students, working moms, singles looking for singles, etc., she could have had a higher chance of success.

Even most websites who are now big, had a small, niche target group they served very well at the very beginning.

Facebook.com started out as a service exclusively for students having an ___@harvard.edu email address, and then expanded to other universities before it was opened to the general public.

Amazon.com started out as an online bookstore focusing mainly on book buyers, but has now created a versatile portfolio of products and is now a global leader in e-commerce.

MensHealth.com started out as a bonus website serving mainly its magazine readers. Now it has not only become an expert website on health issues but also upgraded its website with free personal fitness tracker software and other cool stuff that deals with the topic of health. It is much easier to send your friends to the website than to buy the magazine, hence it now has a much broader online audience than it originally planned.

For you the same rule goes: To make your next product or service a success, you need to fully understand your target group.

Whenever I create a workshop or coaching program I always have the participants in mind. I have, for example, created multiple customized presentation programs for various types of audiences ranging from executives to engineers to small-medium-size business owners to marketing professionals to expert trainers.

For our innovation programs my team and I have customized our training for product designers, marketers, and franchise store operators. We've had to also customize to accomodate mixed groups from multiple departments in one session, to clients focusing on process innovation, etc.

Each program had different requirements so each program required us to prepare differently.

We've come to learn through these and other endeavors that the only time the users really say "WOW" about a product or service is when we truly understand them and their specific needs.

You should aim for the same!

You need to create a demographic and psychographic analysis for all of your users to determine what they want and why they would buy it.

Before you innovate always make sure that you know WHO your target user is. The more you understand your target users, the higher the chance that you will create a successful innovation.

Let's have a look at the second key to understanding clients...

Innovation into Action

Who are your ideal users? Describe them in detail:

_____

_____

_____

_____

_____

_____

Problems & Unmet Needs

"It's not that I'm so smart, it's just that I stay with problems longer."

Albert Einstein

Understanding your ideal user is important, but not enough to create an innovation. To create an innovation you need to understand your ideal user AND you need to find out what innovation they want (or might be interested in buying).

The best way to find out what's wanted and needed is to determine your target users' problems and unmet needs.

Ask yourself: What problems do your ideal users experience? What needs are unmet through your product or service?

Innovations are mainly the solutions to a problem or an unmet need.

> ## Innovations are mainly the solutions to a problem or an unmet need.

Without knowing the problem or unmet need you will have a hard time innovating at all.

Why? Because you end up doing what most companies do: guessing.

The tricky part here is that asking clients what they want or need directly won't necessarily bear fruit, simply because they often don't know themselves (it's your job as an innovator to find out).

Steve Jobs says that often people don't know what they want until you show it to them.

I agree with that!

Asking them what they want will bring few results.

What will bring you big results is asking things like: What are your problems with our product or service? What do you dislike about our product or service? What annoys you about our product or service?

People often don't know what they WANT, but they most certainly know what they do NOT WANT.

Once you figure out what they do NOT WANT, you can start innovating. You now have an opportunity to find a solution and create an even more outstanding product.

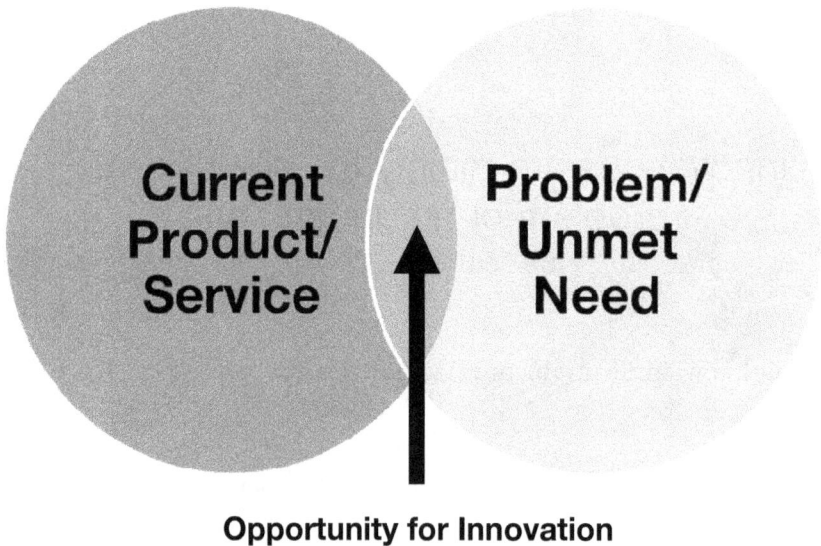

Current Product/ Service

Problem/ Unmet Need

Opportunity for Innovation

Here are a few examples of companies who have found solutions to problems and unmet needs (examples point out only one benefit of each product, regardless of whether it was intended by the inventor or not):

Apple realized that most people hate carrying bulky mp3 players in their pockets, hence they made sure their iPod was both light and slim.

The TV show 'The Biggest Loser' was created to meet the need of over-sized people to get back to their ideal weight within about 10 weeks. The show serves as an inspiration to millions (and of course for the TV channel to gain high viewership).

Porsche knew that many people loved sports cars, but that not everybody could afford them. So they created the Porsche Boxster, a much more affordable version compared to their other models in late 1996.

Jay Sorenson realized that many drinkers of take-out coffee burn their fingers when holding their take-out cups, so he invented the coffee cup sleeve in 1993.

Problem	Unmet Need	Solution
MP3 players takes up too much space	Need for Comfort	Apple iPod
Lots of people in the USA are overweight	Need for Inspiration to lose weight	'The Biggest Loser' TV Show
Luxury sports cars are way too expensive	Need for Affordability	Porsche Boxster
Take-out cups are far too hot to hold	Need for a safe way to hold cup.	The coffee cup sleeve

Look at the above examples, they all show a solution to a problem or unmet need that was based on some sort of inconvenience.

And the inconvenience can be even just a slight discomfort, but if it is a big enough issue for enough people, you know you have a great opportunity for an innovation.

Look out for problems. Look out for unmet needs. Look out for any sort of inconvenience your end users may be experiencing.

They are the true source for great innovation!

Let's have a look at why problems and inconveniences are so important...

Innovation into Action

What are your ideal user's unmet needs or problems?

_____

_____

_____

_____

_____

_____

_____

Why People Buy Anything...

"People don't buy for logical reasons."

Zig Ziglar, famous sales author, expert and speaker

Do you know why your target users will buy your product or service?

It is important for you to understand from the very beginning why people will buy. Understanding this will make sure that you and everyone else on your innovation team knows exactly what to create.

Let's have a look at a simple example.

Can you remember the last time you bought a bottle of water?

What interests me is not what you bought, but why you actually bought it.

Fiji water is 10 times more expensive than regular water. Does that mean Fiji water is also 10 times more healthy? Probably not.

Yet the price is VERY different.

Why do people buy the more expensive water, even though the health benefits are not that significant?

Logically it doesn't make sense, does it?

And this is exactly my point.

Logically it doesn't make sense, but emotionally it does.

Why do people buy anything?

Because of the way it makes them FEEL.

> # People buy your product or service because of the way it makes them FEEL.

Most of the time, we buy what we want, not what we need.

All great marketers are aware of this. It's time now that everyone else also become more aware of this.

People tend to buy because of emotion first, and only then do they back up their purchase with logic.

Why would someone spend more than double the money for a Porsche Cayenne versus a VW Touareg even though they come from the same factory in Germany and are basically the same car?

Because of the way it makes them feel.

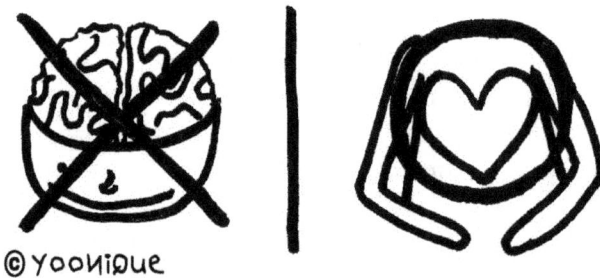

© yoonique

The Porsche Cayenne makes them feel richer, more successful, more able, more confident, special, different, and so on.

Unfortunately, the way companies create products or services and then market them is often the inverse of this:

Product Creation   ⇨   **Features**   ⇨   **Benefits**
(LOGIC)   **(EMOTIONS)**

120

First they create the product, and while creating they focus on creating features and later the marketing department of the company figures out what benefits will urge people to buy it.

They start with LOGIC and then proceed to EMOTION.

What if the all the inventors out there understood this principle? Do you think they could create a more benefit-focused product for their users? You bet!

From now on whenever you are creating a product or service, I want you to think about it in the following way:

Benefits ⇨ **Features** ⇨ **Product Creation**
(EMOTIONS) **(LOGIC)**

First think of the benefits for the client (emotional benefits especially), and then think of what features might bring your ideal user these benefits, and ONLY then start creating.

This way, you can be sure to create something of higher value to the client, plus your marketing will be simpler and faster.

Later in Step 4: Innovation Marketing, you will learn more about how to create effective benefits and benefit statements for you to turn your products or services into innovations.

For now keep one thing in mind: Focus on what people WANT to buy.

Focus on what people WANT to buy.

Innovation into Action

Look back at the PROBLEMS or UNMET NEEDS your wrote down in the last chapter. Make a note of what the ideal emotional benefit of solving those problems or unmet needs is:

_____

_____

_____

_____

_____

Competitors

"I have no friends and no enemies – only competitors."

Aristotle Onassis, Greek shipping magnate

Copying or benchmarking competitors is one of the worst things to do! In fact it is the exact opposite of innovation.

Understanding competitors to create great innovations though can serve as a great inspiration and motivator for you (especially if the competition creates beautiful products and services).

> ## Use your competitors as an inspiration or to find mistakes you can fix.

Let's face it. If you've ever played sports, you know that the fastest way to become better and better is to find an opponent who is one level above you and practice with him or her.

Sometimes it can be similar with innovation. Look at competitors for inspiration to move to the next level. To move ahead. To get to the next step.

One thing I admired when I trained Microsoft employees in the past was that they openly admitted that they loved the new Apple iPod nano (which had just come out at the time) and used it as inspiration to create simpler and more stylish products and services.

That's probably one of the reasons why Microsoft is one of the world's most innovative companies (they were ranked 4th in BusinessWeek's annual list in 2009). They use competitors as a means of inspiration not jealousy.

You should do the same! Don't copy. Don't be jealous. But think about how to create at the next level.

In order to use competitors to create more innovative products or services you should focus on the following 3 standards:

a. Mistake: "Do they make any mistakes that we could fix?"

If they make a mistake that users don't like, gives them discomfort or is an unmet need and you can fix it, you just found another great opportunity for an innovation.

In 2000, lots of people bought small-sized cars.

At that time Volkswagen was doing well, but had more competitors than ever before in its history: from Italy (Fiat), France (Renault) and especially Japan (Mitsubishi, Honda, etc.).

What was Volkswagen's solution to stand out from the crowd?

They focused on a mistake all competitors made: Almost all small cars were cost-saving and hence unattractive and unappealing.

What was Volkswagen's solution?

They decided to update an old design, the new Volkswagen "Beetle" not only drew on a rich history, it was also more attractive and appealing

By focusing all their marketing on a small market that was ready for the next car revolution, i.e. people who loved the old beetle model, VW managed to penetrate the broader market too by attracting people who loved small cars but were more interested in stylish models rather than the standard cost-saving models.

b. Niche – "Did they overlook a niche market that we could capitalize on?"

The second thing to ask yourself is whether they have overlooked a niche market. Many companies can only focus their products on so many niche markets.

Have you ever heard of Bikram Yoga?

Bikram Yoga was invented by Bikram Choudhury in the 1970s. Another name for it is 'hot yoga'. The difference between regular yoga and Bikram Yoga is that Bikram Yoga is performed in a 40.5 degree (105 Fahrenheit) room.

The hot room helps accelerates weight loss.

The niche market Bikram Yoga focuses on are overweight people, who want to lose weight fast. Hardcore exercisers who want to see results faster.

Bikram Yoga focuses on a smaller niche market that doesn't match the mainstream and fixes a problem faster for a big chunk of the yoga market, and that's why it became world famous and successful.

c. Standard – "Have they introduced a new industry standard that we need to follow?"

Remember the case of the Sony Betamax? How they were the only ones who used their new system, but all the other companies in the world chose VHS?

Sony would have been smarter studying the trends of their competitors and innovating on VHS, OR should have found a way to make their system the leading one.

Creating the industry standard is of course the ideal, but if you lack the timing or the talent for that, at least your company is in alignment with the rest of the industry and can innovate better based on whichever new standard has emerged.

Before you start to innovate on your next product or service, have a look at your largest competitors to check if they have made any mistakes that you can capitalize on, find a niche they're overlooking or if they're setting a new standard.

Either way, do not use them for copying and benchmarking, but to move in a different (and more innovative) direction than they have.

Innovation into Action

Who is your main competitor? Rate them using the 3 keys we discussed:

Competitor: _____

a. Mistakes: _____

b. Niche: _____

c. Standard: _____

Trend Forecasting

"The genius of investing is recognizing the direction of a trend - not catching highs and lows."

Source Unknown

For you to create innovations and solve problems or unmet needs, it is good to know what's going on in the world.

New trends emerge daily.

The more you know about and understand how trends emerge and spread, the easier it will be to create your own.

And I'm not talking just about trends in your direct industry, but also understanding trends in other industries, because often the greatest innovations are created when ideas from another industry are transferred to your own.

How can you stay on top of what's going on in the trend department? Have a look at the following tips and choose at least one that you want to turn into a weekly or at least monthly habit to stay on top of trends that are going on:

a. Trend Websites & Blogs

Probably the easiest and fastest way to find out about new trends is online. Using trend websites and blogs, you can check out what is going on around the world, and inside and outside of your industry.

Here are some trend websites I recommend you have a look at:

www.trendhunter.com The #1 website on trends with over 8 million monthly views, they feature 47,000 micro-trends and cutting edge ideas.

www.trendsresearch.com Website by Gerald Celente, the World's #1 Trends Forecaster who has been featured on Oprah, CNN, New York Post, Fox, etc.

www.smallbiztrends.com Online, award-winning publication focusing on Small Business Trends.

www.psfk.com Trends from around the world in popular, consumer and business culture.

www.trendcentral.com Trends from around the world on Lifestyle, Style, Entertainment and Technology.

www.trendwatching.com Trends from hundreds of spotters from more than 120 countries worldwide.

www.google.com/zeitgeist Look into search trends at Google from all around the world.

web-japan.org/trends Japanese Trends on fashion, lifestyle, sci-tech, pop culture and food & travel.

www.trendguide.com Trends from electronics to shoes to accessories to industrial design to styling to art.

www.trends.com Website selling journals with trends on biochemical sciences, biotechnology, cell biology, genetics, neurosciences, etc.

b. Magazines

Certain magazines cover trends all the time. Look for magazines inside or outside your industry that show signs of "NEW", "IDEAS", "INNOVATIONS", "TRENDS" and other similar words on the cover.

Some magazines are clearly ahead of others in terms of trends and new ideas. Focus on these and you'll find new trends.

c. Books that focus on trends

Check out books on trends. Numerous books come out each year with new trends from all over the world.

There are books explaining trends in general, some that come out every year, and some that are industry specific. All of them can help you understand trends better.

d. Trade Shows & Conferences

Visit trade shows and conferences. They can either be related to your industry or not. Go to those that talk about the future or new products or services in your industry.

f. TV

Many trends can be spotted on TV, either in commercials or on TV shows. Try watching shows that always show something new and give you a new look at trends and interesting things that are happening.

g. Try Something New

As discussed earlier in this book, try something new. The more new things you try and the more new things you see and experience, the easier it will be to spot trends in various industries.

All these experiences will not only be beneficial but will also help you to master Part 2: Innovation Tools, where we will discuss how to come up with superior ideas to the problems or unmet needs you've identified.

The 6 Problem Finders

Finding problems and unmet needs is important. Knowing how to find them might be even more important. Here are seven ways to find hot buttons in your industry:

> ## Knowing how to find problems is a key skill of great innovators.

1. Extreme End Users

Asking the end user is often the easiest and fastest way to figure out what it is that they want.

Makes sense, doesn't it?! If you want to know what problems people have with a car, ask someone who uses it all the time.

Actually it's not that easy.

Many product managers from large companies will actually tell you that asking the users what they want is the stupidest thing you can do.

As I mentioned earlier, Steve Jobs said "Most people don't know what they want until you show it to them."

131

And it's true. Asking a user "What do you want?" will either lead to a blank stare or some funny answers that for the most part don't help you (most people are expert buyers, not expert innovators).

Instead of asking them "What do you want?", ask them "What's a problem you're experiencing with the product or service? What annoys you? What's not perfect about the product or service?"

Trust me, these questions get people talking!

And this way you can figure out what their problems and unmet needs are. Then your job is of course to create a solution for the problem in terms of your next innovation.

© yoonique

2. Hater End Users

Ask users who actually hate your product.

Remember our InnoBasics lesson: Ask people who disagree with you.

The only thing you need to remember to ask people who hate your product to focus on are the FACTS.

Don't accept complaints. Don't accept bitching. Accept facts and facts only.

Years ago, I had a lady in my Presentation Latte™ workshop who didn't like the workshop at all, while everyone else in the room loved it.

Everyone learned, practiced and delivered with passion and excitement, while she sat through the whole course with a grumpy face.

At the end of the workshop I asked her what it was she didn't like. She ended up giving me a 30 minute feedback session (interesting how one little question can sometimes trigger this kind of response).

The feedback I got was 80% useless and had to do with her attitude, but the 20% that were facts were actually very useful for me to develop and improve the workshop even further.

To this day I appreciate the feedback. It helped my team and I create an even better workshop.

3. The Expert

Another way to discover problems or unmet needs is to ask experts who use (or fix or sell or train on) your product or service daily.

Experts often get complaints from people in the industry. They are the direct channel between the product or service and the end user.

One conversation with a true expert will lead to a lot of insight, trust me.

Often you have to invest a little more money for that, but if you choose the right expert and ask the right questions it can be worthwhile.

Before starting to write books, for example, I interviewed multiple authors on how they did it, and what problems they encountered, while treating them to lunch.

Trust me I learned more in a few hours over lunch about the publishing industry than I could have learned studying it from the outside for a year.

4. Focus Groups

How about getting a room full of users?

That's what focus groups are all about. You get a group of users, ask them to test your product or service together with you in the room and later they give you feedback about what went wrong.

The advantage of this method is that you can get tons of feedback in a short period of time. Also, sometimes groups tend to spin their problems further after they hear other members' problems.

The potential danger is that the group has one leader who dominates with his or her ideas and all the others follow (that way you waste time and get unsatisfying results).

I once conducted a focus group feedback session for a major client, and that's exactly what happened.

We had a group of about 12 people, yet the whole room was dominated by the first guy who was so strong and opinionated that the others in the room felt uncomfortable going against his ideas.

If you encounter a similar situation, let the "dominator" speak last. Simply tell all focus group members that you will change the order and do it in a way that he or she can share last.

5. Competitors

Yes, you're reading correctly. Meet your competitors and check out the mistakes that they're making. If possible, even ask them.

The second best option is to study their products or services by buying or joining.

Again, you do NOT do this for benchmarking, you do it to see what mistakes they are making and what niches and problems they're overlooking.

6. Look-in-the-Mirror

How does Apple create its products? They focus on creating products THEY like.

If they like their products, then they're doing something right.

What they mean is that sometimes the best user is yourself. That sometimes the best person to figure out problems in your industry is you.

Ask yourself: What is it that you don't like about your product or service?

On a scale from 1 to 10 how would you rate your own product or service? If it's not a 10, WHY NOT?

That's another easy way to figure out problems you or your competitors might be overlooking.

Innovation into Action

Which of the 6 Problem Finders will you apply for your current project? (Check)

a. Extreme End Users _____

b. Hater End Users _____

c. The Expert _____

d. Target Groups _____

e. Competitors _____

f. Look-in-the-Mirror _____

Step 2

InnoTools

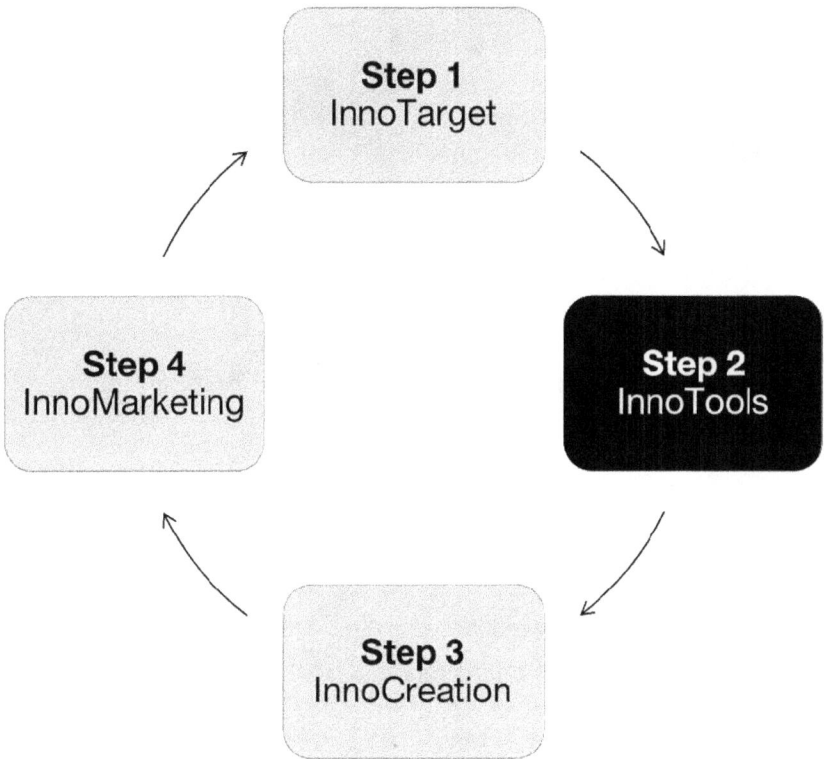

Step 1
InnoTarget

Step 2
InnoTools

Step 3
InnoCreation

Step 4
InnoMarketing

Got Ideas?

Are you creative? Innovative? An idea person? A brainstormer?

One of the keys to coming up with new ideas is brainstorming.

So, simply to test your current level of abilities, I'd like to you to use the blank pages below.

Think of the problem or need you defined for your user in the last chapter and brainstorm as many ideas as you can to solve that problem or cover that need.

You should be able to do so in less than 30 minutes.

Some Ground Rules: Make sure you come up with lots and lots of ideas. Make sure ALL your ideas are creative and could be the next global bestseller.

With that said…30 minutes…and GO!

(Did you really do it??? If not go back and do it NOW. If you don't, you'll miss out on learning an important lesson. And if you read on you'll miss out on a WOW moment. Last chance!)

How did you do?

How many ideas did you come up with?

Quickly count and write down how many you came up with in the box below:

Were they all creative and did they have the potential to turn your product, service or business into a global bestseller? Write down all the ideas that you think have the potential to be guaranteed bestsellers in this next box:

Take a quick look at your results.

Do you think you came up with lots of ideas, or with too few?

Did you feel burdened that ALL your ideas had to be successful?

The above exercise shows how most people approach brainstorming or coming up with new ideas.

Bad strategy!

For most people the scariest thing in the world is a BLANK SHEET of paper on which they have to create something new (in my opinion this fear comes a close second to the fear of public speaking).

The reasons for this are simple:

1. They don't know (or don't apply) the FAIR RULES of brainstorming.

2. They don't have a brainstorming SYSTEM (quite frankly great brainstormers can fill up a blank sheet of paper only because they have a system – a set of brainstorming techniques – that works well every time.)

In this chapter you will learn exactly that: the rules of brainstorming as well as multiple brainstorming methods that give you a system that makes coming up with new ideas effortless.

Why **Step 2:** InnoTools?!

From InnoTarget to InnoTools

In Step 1: InnoTarget you determined your ideal users and their problems and unmet needs. You should now have a clear target to aim for.

In Step 2: InnoTools will give you the tools to come up with lots of ideas to solve the problems and unmet needs you've defined in step 1.

The Problem in a Nutshell

Most people are scared to death.

They are scared to death by a rather normal and non-threatening thing.

It's the BLANK SHEET of paper.

The little blank sheet of paper scares a lot of people.

Giving them a blank sheet and telling them: "Here. Come up with as many ideas as possible in 2 hours" can be hell for many people.

The Purpose of InnoTools

> The purpose of InnoTools is to give you tools that make it EASY to master that BLANK SHEET and come up with lots of ideas in a short time.

You will learn multiple tools for various situations and various people that are easy to apply and most importantly instantly learnable by pretty much anyone.

These InnoTools are what your team should use anytime they need to come up with ideas and solutions to your InnoTargets.

When to Use InnoTools

AFTER you've defined your InnoTarget and are ready to come up with lots of ideas to solve the problems and unmet needs you've identified.

Get ready to learn the InnoTools!

Brainstorming Rules

"An idea that is not dangerous is unworthy of being called an idea at all."

Oscar Wilde

Brainstorming was originally invented in 1930 by Alex Faickney Osborn and is still one of the most popular creativity techniques used today.

Brainstorming happens when 2 or more people get together to think of ideas to solve a problem.

Even though brainstorming is very famous, many people often forget its basic rules, so here they are:

© yoonique

1. Define the Problem!

I said it in the last chapter and I have to say it again: without a specific problem to solve your brainstorming is often a waste of time. Make sure that your problem is clearly defined.

For example, instead of focusing on 'creating a new car' focus on something like "How can we create a car that does NOT destroy the environment?" (that's probably how hybrid cars came about).

2. Focus on quantity

The goal of brainstorming is to get as many ideas as possible on paper. The more ideas the better. The more ideas your team generates, the higher the chances are that at some point, you will come up with an idea that's a winner.

3. Withhold criticism

In the brainstorming stage, being critical is forbidden. Everyone must feel free to share ideas without being criticized. Criticism prevents good ideas from being expressed. Ideas can be evaluated and criticized at a later stage.

4. Welcome wild ideas

The wilder the ideas, the better. The more people are encouraged to think in different directions, the higher the chances are that you can come up with a new, unique idea that's a winner.

5. Connect and improve ideas

When you hear someone else's idea and you have an idea that's related or better, say it. You want to build on others' ideas. The goal is to constantly come up with better ideas while building on others.

6. Be Visual

Use colored post-its. Use colored pens. Draw. Use pictures. Use cutouts from magazines. The more visual, the better it is for your right brain (the creative side you want to stimulate especially during brainstorming).

I personally like to draw, show pictures or highlight important ideas with colors and big letters. You might want to do something similar to make your brainstorming more successful.

7. One Conversation at a Time

This rule doesn't apply to everyone and to all groups, but I've found that in my experience of running creativity workshops, especially talkative groups need to follow this rule.

Have one conversation at a time. Brainstorming doesn't mean that all people blurt out their ideas all at once. Give people a chance to finish what they have to say. If someone has an idea while another person is talking, encourage them to write the idea down and wait their turn to speak.

If you have a particularly unruly team, it can be good to use a prop such as a ball or pen. The person, and ONLY the person, holding the ball or pen is allowed to talk.

I strongly recommend that every time you start a brainstorming session, you start by reminding people of these rules.

Even though most people think they know them, they often don't act on them once the brainstorming really begins.

In my team for example, if we don't remind each other not to criticize ahead of a brainstorming session, everyone starts evaluating and criticizing an idea immediately, based on its feasibility.

So, to avoid someone being criticized or made fun of (which inhibits people from speaking up), make sure you run through the rules at the beginning of each brainstorming session.

Another important tip is WHO to include in your brainstorming sessions.

I recommend you choose all different types of people who have very different perspectives. Even though it might be more challenging to manage the personalities involved, you'll get a more unique blend of ideas, and that's exactly what you want.

Think again of the 11 InnoTypes. Ideally you're looking to get ideas from all different InnoTypes.

Here's the summarized list of brainstorming rules. Print them out and put them on your wall or on a card in the middle of your brainstorming table.

BRAINSTORMING RULES

1. Define the Problem

2. Focus on Quantity

3. Withhold Criticism

4. Welcome Wild Ideas

5. Connect & Improve Ideas

6. Be Visual

7. One Conversation at a Time

Great innovators use brainstorming as one of their strongest tools. They remind their team of the rules. They choose people who have different backgrounds and opinions. They generate better ideas than they expected.

In the rest of this chapter you will learn various advanced brainstorming techniques.

Innovation into Action

Print out the brainstorming rules and put them somewhere you can see them during your brainstorming sessions. If your brainstorming sessions tend to change venue frequently remember to print them out and bring them along.

Number Brainstorming

"Talent is a matter of quantity. Talent does not write one page, it writes three hundred."

Jules Renard

If I asked you to come up with more than 500 different ways to use a brick right now, could you do it?

Even though people do brainstorming many of them still have a hard time doing it or find it difficult to come up with enough ideas.

Quantity seems to be a particular problem that people face when brainstorming.

Most people harbor a mistaken belief that there are only so many ideas they can come up with and once they've reached that limit, they simply give up.

But if they had persisted, they would have come up with some truly winning ideas.

One strategy that helps to solve this problem is to simply predetermine how many ideas you have to come up with in your brainstorming session.

If, for example, I told you to come up with as many ways to package a product as possible, how many would you come up with?

Maybe 20? Maybe 40?

But, what if I told you to come up with 200 ways to package a product right now? Could you do it?

Of course you could! You might not like doing it, but you could come up with 200 answers.

The mind is designed to give you an answer to any problem you give it.

This is why you should decide at the beginning of your brainstorming session how many ideas you want to come up with!

Do you want to come up with 20? 100? 500? 1,000? 10,000?

Decide ahead of time!

In our workshops we ask our participants to brainstorm at least 1,000 ideas or more in a few short hours.

© yoonique

As you can imagine, most of them sit there incredulous, thinking "Are you kidding me?"

Interestingly though, all our workshop participants are able to live up to the challenge by the end.

Is it tough? Yes! Is it challenging? Yes! Do they complete the job anyway? Yes, they do!

You might be asking yourself now: "Ben, are you saying that restrictions lead to creativity?" My answer to you is: "Yes, they absolutely do!"

The famous author T.S. Eliot once said that:

"When forced to work within a strict framework the imagination is taxed to its utmost – and will produce its richest ideas. Given total freedom the work is likely to sprawl."

Restriction leads to freedom. And the easiest way to do it, is to simply come up with an outrageous number before you start brainstorming.

Again, the goal of brainstorming is to come up with as many ideas as possible. By setting yourself a big number of ideas to brainstorm before you start, you stand a greater chance of coming up with some winning ideas.

So, next time you brainstorm give yourself and your team a target number of ideas that you need to come up with. Chances are high you will get more ideas than if you just said 'as many ideas as possible'.

Great innovators set themselves a target number of ideas to come up with before they start brainstorming.

Innovation into Action

How many ideas will come up with in your next brainstorming session? 10 ideas? 100? 1,000? 10,000?

Write down your number here: _____

ABC Brainstorming

"Why is the alphabet in that order? Is it because of that song? The guy who wrote that song wrote everything."

Steven Wright
American Actor & Writer

How is our language organized? Using the ALPHABET!

How do we think? In pictures (right brain) and the ABC (left brain).

(If you speak a different language, simply exchange the ABC for whatever system matches the ABC in your language. My Korean trainers have substituted the ABC for Korean *Hangul* in their training/consulting.)

One of the best ways to brainstorm is to use the ABC to its full potential.

As I mentioned earlier all the associations in our brain are a connection of words (left brain) and pictures (right brain).

Since almost all brainstorming happens using words, the ABC can be used to great effect. It gives you a minimum of 26 ideas for each problem that you need to solve.

I learned this method from German brain-expert Vera F. Birkenbihl (whose books and work I highly recommend!).

The reason ABC Brainstorming works so well, is because all information in your brain is organized alphabetically. So if you want to come up with new ideas, it's excellent to draw on all the things that are available to you.

Also, using the ABC is a great way to connect ideas.

For example, if I asked you to 'Brainstorm Big Companies' it might probably take you some time, but using the ABC Brainstorming technique you could come up with names much, much faster.

A pple	J & J	S amsung
B MW	K rispy Kreme	T iffany's
C isco Systems	L G	U nited Airlines
D aimler	M cDonalds	V odafone
E pson	N ike	W al-Mart
F ila	O ffice Depot	X erox
G oogle	P rada	Y ahoo
H ead	Q ualcomm	Z egna
I BM	R oyal Dutch Shell	

Another example: If I told you to brainstorm '26 Ways to Get More Clients' using the ABC, your list could look something like this:

A dvertising	J oin groups	S end Postcards
B illboards	K eep cool	T rain sales team
C alling	L ists of clients	U tilize others
D ifferentiation	M arketing	V isualize results
E xecute plan	N egotiate, network	W ork smart
F ire losers	O utsell competitors	X ray your system
G oal-setting	P recall planning	Y ear-end party

H ire winners	Q uestion more	Z igzag to success
I nitiate conversations	R eflect after meet	

Another example: If I told you to brainstorm '26 Words to Describe YOU' using the ABC, your list could look something like this:

A wesome	J ack-of-all-trades	S exy
B old	K nowledgeable	T rendy
C aring	L ovely	U nique
D reamer	M essy	V aluable
E nergetic	N ice	W inner
F un	O pen-minded	X mas-loving
G orgeous	P owerful	Y ours truly
H ilarious	Q uestioning	Z esty!
I nteresting	R ational	

© yoouique

As you can see, the ABC Brainstorming technique will help you come up with more ideas than you considered possible.

It becomes especially interesting when you have a couple of empty spots to fill in and you check the dictionary for other words or ideas.

155

You can easily do ABC Brainstorming by yourself if you cannot find anyone to do it with. Also it is great to pass it around and get others' input.

All you have to do is carry it around with you and pull it out whenever you meet someone. Get their perspective. Add their ideas to your list. (by the way, each letter can have more than 1 answer, some of my lists have had up to 15 answers per letter).

Now it's your turn: Try to brainstorm great names for a new cell phone.

A	J	S
B	K	T
C	L	U
D	M	V
E	N	W
F	O	X
G	P	Y
H	Q	Z
I	R	

One more time: Brainstorm what the NEXT LEVEL coffee shop might look like. (What will be the next big thing in the retail beverage industry?)

A	J	S
B	K	T
C	L	U
D	M	V
E	N	W
F	O	X
G	P	Y
H	Q	Z
I	R	

ABC Brainstorming is easy to learn and easy to master, and best of all it can really help you brainstorm faster and get more ideas. One more way to use ABC Brainstorming is to determine the letter you want to find many words for.

For example, when I wrote my book 'Presentation Latte', I decided that I wanted all the principles to start with a **P**, because many words that related to presentations start with a **P**.

The result after a few days of brainstorming and reordering were the following 7½ P's:

P1 – People

P2 – Passion

P3 – Purpose

P4 – Preparation

P5 – Presence

P6 – Participation

P7 – Power

P7½ – PowerPoint

The feedback I got from readers was that the book felt organized in a very creative way, and was easy to remember because all the points started with a *P*.

And there's no reason why you can't do the same.

Great Innovators use ABC Brainstorming to take their brainstorming to the next level.

Old + Old Brainstorming

"There are no new ideas."

Audre Lorde

Let's do a little test here. What do you get when you add the following products together?

Latte	**+**	**Green tea**	**=**	**?**
TV	**+**	**3D**	**=**	**?**
Webcams	**+**	**Meetings**	**=**	**?**
Pizza	**+**	**Home Delivery**	**=**	**?**

The products I'm talking about are of course Green Tea Latte, 3D Televisions, teleconferencing and Pizza Delivery service. Innovations that are now standard for most people in developed countries (except 3D TVs).

One of the ways in which innovative products and services are created is by connecting 2 or more OLD products or ideas together. That's why this brainstorming technique is called 'Old + Old'.

We will get into this in greater detail later on in this chapter when we talk about "The Inno18" brainstorming technique, but for now let's first master a simplified version of this technique.

To start with, don't forget most NEW things are really only a connection of several OLD things. The only difference is how we connect these old things to each other.

One exercise that we do with the participants of our Innovation Workshop is that we practice this strategy.

The result is almost always fantastic. Using the Old + Old Brainstorming Technique, participants who are usually not very good at coming up with great ideas, get incredible results within only a few minutes of brainstorming with their team.

Try it out yourself next time you're brainstorming. Get your product or write down your service and think about which product or service you could connect it with to create an innovative idea.

One of my personal favorites is to put the product on my desk and place the other products I'd like to combine it with next to it. That way I can always see it in front of me and my mind works almost on autopilot creating new ideas.

One of the other speakers at a recent conference that I spoke at in Korea was an 18-year old software programmer. Needless to say he was the youngest presenter in the room.

He was the creator of "Seoul Bus", an App for smart phones that shows users when their bus will arrive using their phone's 3G service.

What old ideas did he connect? A smartphone + Seoul Bus Map + government bus control system (which tracks where any bus is at any given moment). He wrapped it all up into one little smartphone App.

The App has been downloaded by more than 400,000 people and counting for the iPhone alone. No small feat considering that the iPhone has only been on the Korean market for 4 months at the time of writing.

One of the best things about this strategy is that it is really fun. You have two or more products or service ideas in front of you and are connecting them in unusual and thought-provoking ways.

From 2in1 Shampoo & Conditioner (shampoo + conditioner) to the Pill Cam (an ingestible pill + a camera + an antenna to scope out people's guts for cancer) to Amazon.com (internet + bookstore), many innovations that exist today were created by combining 2 or more old items or ideas.

Great innovators constantly think of how they can connect two or more products or services.

Innovation into Action

What are 2 or 3 products or services that you can combine with your own?

_____ + _____ + _____ = _____

_____ + _____ + _____ = _____

_____ + _____ + _____ = _____

Magazine Brainstorming

Magazine Brainstorming requires you to use various magazines.

It works best as a supplement to Old + Old brainstorming because it helps you think up possible product or service ideas that connect with your current product or service.

@yoonique

To magazine brainstorm follow these basics steps:

1. Define your problem

As always, start by defining the problem you have to brainstorm about and find a solution for.

2. Get various magazines

Get various magazines from various sectors and industries. Often industries outside of your own can inspire you to come up with truly unique and innovative ideas. Where possible, choose magazines that have more pictures than text. In addition to magazines consider going through catalogs that sometimes have a bigger variety of products.

3. Flip through them

Very quickly flip through all of them. Do NOT read. Just look at the pictures and think if you could possibly connect them with your product or service. The key here is speed.

4. Rip out ideas

Rip out anything that has even the slightest chance of being connected with your product or service. Even if you're unsure just rip it out anyway. You can decide later whether it's really useful or not.

It can be quite useful to rip out your ideas and put them up on the wall with some tape. Later you can reshuffle them to form a wall mind map (more on mind maps later).

5. Connect ideas

Put the ideas that you've ripped out next to your current product or service and ask yourself how you can connect them. Brainstorm multiple ideas on your own or with your team.

Lots of advertising experts use a similar technique when they have to come up with new advertising.

They rip out multiple ads they like, tape them to the wall and circle the parts they like the most and which they could use as inspiration in their new advertising.

Another version of magazine brainstorming which I sometimes use is what I like to call *TV Brainstorming*.

In *TV Brainstorming* you flip through various channels quickly and write down any ideas that you see on the screen in commercials, shows or movies that you could connect and brainstorm about.

Sometimes when I'm stuck with a problem or an idea I go to the nearest bookstore or coffee shop to flip through magazines that I don't usually read (or never read at all).

Often by the end, the solutions or ideas or options naturally come to me and I ask myself "Why didn't I think of this before?"

Great innovators use magazines (sometimes even TV) for their brainstorming sessions to help inspire them and to help them to visualize ideas.

Innovation into Action

Which magazines could you use for Magazine Brainstorming? Try it out! It's fun.

_____

60-Second Brainstorming

Another great way to brainstorm is what I call the *60-Second Brainstorming* technique.

I originally learned the idea from Vera F. Birkenbihl, the well-known German expert in the areas of creativity, memory and self-development.

The *60-Second Brainstorming* technique works as follows:

Imagine I sit with you for dinner and tell you about a problem I need new ideas for.

What usually happens next? You will probably talk to me for the next hour or so about ways I can solve the problem that you back with stories and examples from your personal experience.

This can be a very long and painful procedure (especially if I have to ask more than 10 people for their ideas).

60-Second Brainstorming can help you cut the 1 hour down to 1 minute.

Here's how to use the strategy successfully:

1. Index Card

Write down the problem or need you want to brainstorm about on a index card. Make it simple and specific, so you can quickly explain it to a person who is not in your line of business in 30 seconds or less.

The more clearly defined your problem or need, the better.

I once had a gentleman in one of my workshops who was unsatisfied with the answers he got from the other participants. I asked him to share his problem with us, and to his own surprise the minute he read it out loud, he realized how unspecific he was being.

Once he clarified his problem to us (and possibly to himself too), several people were able to give him some answers that addressed his problem in a meaningful and applicable way.

Make sure your problem or need is clear and specific!

2. Choose the Person

Find a person whose brain you want to pick. Show them your card and explain the problem or goal you are brainstorming ideas for.

Choose people from various fields and backgrounds. Sometimes outsiders have better ideas than people closer to home.

3. 60-Second Time Limit

Tell him or her that this is a little game of intelligence. You want to see how many great ideas he or she can come up in 60-seconds or less. Pull out your watch to show that you are serious about the time limit.

4. Key Words Only

To make the time count, explain that they shouldn't go into detail; they should express their ideas using keywords only. Tell them that if you need more details, you will ask for them later.

That way you make sure that you get all the other person's ideas on the table in 60 seconds or less.

5. Write Down the Ideas You Hear

As the person with whom you are brainstorming shares their ideas, write them down. Write down keywords only. Write quickly, and legibly.

6. Next Person

After you have heard all the possible ideas and you're happy with the result, you can move on to the next person to pick his or her brain.

If you test it out, you will discover that many people will not even be able to go for the full 60 seconds. Most people stop generating ideas about a topic at around 40 seconds.

For example if I asked you to brainstorm ideas for a 'new package for a beverage' and I asked you for all the ideas you could come up with in 60 seconds, could you last the full 60 seconds?

Try it out right now!

Ready?

Ok. 60 seconds…and go!

© yoonique

Plastic bottle.

Glass bottle.

Paper cup.

Can.

Different size bottles (4L, 2L, 1L, 500ml, 250ml, 100ml).

Coffee cup.

Boxed instead of round.

Bottle made of wood.

Small plastic bag.

You probably couldn't come up with more than 15 answers.

That's what happens with normal people on a specialized topic. They run out of ideas after about 40 seconds.

BUT the great news is that by asking multiple people from multiple backgrounds, you usually get multiple new ideas (if you ask 20 people and get 15 ideas from each of them, that's 300 ideas in 20 minutes) that you can brainstorm further on, and chances are will lead you to come up with a couple of great ones.

During one of our open innovation seminars we had a young engineer who had a pressing problem for the product he'd created.

When we did the 60-Second Brainstorming exercise with everyone and he got a chance to ask more than 10 people, not only was the problem solved, but he said afterwards that he'd gotten even more ideas to further upgrade his product.

Are you ready? 60 seconds...and go!

Innovation into Action

Get an index card. Write down your problem and carry it around with you. Then when you meet people, pull out the card and ask them for their ideas to your problem. Ask at least 5 people today, then write down the best ideas you got here:

_____

_____

_____

Top-to-Bottom Brainstorming

Imagine you worked in the R&D department of a large company. Your job is to come up with a brand-new, innovative product and you need to collect ideas from many other people.

If I gave you the option, who would you ask for their ideas: The CEO of the company or the lowest level maintenance guy?

Which one would you choose?

Most people would probably choose the CEO because of their experience. Some people might choose the maintenance guy.

Who would I choose? BOTH!

> ## Great innovators get ideas from uncommon sources.

Top-to-Bottom Brainstorming is all about asking everyone in your company (and outside of it) for their ideas.

Everyone, yes everyone, might have a great idea for your project.

The key is to get as much input as possible.

If you only ask high-level people, chances are you will get similar results. But if you ask people from different positions or different departments, or even different companies, you will get completely different ideas.

The best brainstormers I've met in my life, always take the opportunity to ask myself and others for our thoughts and ideas on things they're working on.

Whenever I meet one of my friends for dinner, he pulls out a card to tell me about a current problem or goal and asks me for my ideas on how to achieve the goal or overcome the problem.

He doesn't only do it with me but with many people.

You too can use the power of Top-to-Bottom Brainstorming. Simply ask everyone you meet for their ideas and feedback.

© yoonique

Sometimes people are embarrassed to ask. Don't be!

People usually love to share their ideas. They love to feel special. They love to feel important. Remember, feeling important is one of our most basic needs as human beings.

Make sure that after you get their ideas, you thank them wholeheartedly regardless of whether their ideas were that great or not. That way they will love to share their ideas with you in the future.

Ask people inside and outside of your department. Ask people inside and outside of your company.

I often work outside the office in coffee shops when I write books or work on other things I create.

During these sessions I sometimes receive or create VISUAL ideas (e.g. book cover, design for marketing material, etc.) or NAME ideas (e.g. names for a new product or service or a general concept idea).

Who do I ask for their opinion? The staff working at the coffee shop!

Even though I don't always get the best feedback, every now and then I get terrific ideas from them. I once got a winning design for a successful marketing campaign that my team created.

As you can see, anyone might have a good idea!

Did you for example know that the person who came up with the name of the 'iPod' was not even an Apple employee?

The name was suggested by Vinnie Chieco, a freelance copywriter, who was inspired by a line from the movie 2001: A Space Odyssey ("Open the pod bay door, HAL.").

As you see, outsiders' ideas can matter as much as ideas that originate within your own company.

Great innovators ask different people from different areas for their ideas.

Innovation into Action

Who are people you have never asked for their opinion? Make a list and ask them:

Person: _____ Ideas: _____

Person: _____ Ideas: _____

Person: _____ Ideas: _____

Person: _____ Ideas: _____

The Inno18

"Combine the extremes, and you will have the true center."

Karl Wilhelm Friedrich Schlegel

Imagine there was a system that would make brainstorming and new products and services easier and faster than any other method...

In the following pages I will share with you the Inno18: 18 Innovation brainstorming strategies to effortlessly create your next innovative product or service.

Of all the brainstorming techniques this is by far the most advanced and probably also the hardest to use. But it is worth mastering.

Most products and services in the world that have become famous innovations have been created using these 18 principles (knowingly or unknowingly).

The key behind each of the principles is a key question you want to ask yourself over and over again.

Just like the Wright Brothers asked themselves "How can we fly?", you'll also want to ask yourself these questions over and over again.

Let's have a look at the Inno18.

Inno1: Speed

People love speed! We live in the 'age of speed'. Everything is going faster, moving faster, and happening faster.

We want our food faster, our dry-cleaning faster, our means of travel faster. In short: we'd like everything done as fast as possible.

Customers expect things to go faster for two reasons: to save time and to save money.

If you can make your product or service faster in some way, you'll have a big advantage assuming that it's not already the standard in your industry.

Some famous SPEED products or services include:

- 3G (faster mobile telecommunication)
- CESSNA Citation X (world's fastest passenger airplane with top speed of Mach 0.92)
- MAGLEV train (high speed train)
- BROADBAND (high-speed internet)
- DOMINO'S PIZZA (fast food delivery; 30 minutes or less)
- DHL EXPRESS WORLDWIDE (you can send a letter from New York City to Seoul in less than 48 hours)
- INSTANT MESSAGING (from Twitter.com to AIM to MSN Messenger)
- SPRAY NAIL ART (covers nails much faster than regular nail varnish)

How could you make YOUR product or service FASTER? Write down your ideas: _____

Inno2: Slowness

People want things to go faster in general, that is true.

But there are also a lot of examples where people want things to go slower.

Speed seems to be everywhere. You hear people complaining that "everything is going too fast".

Many people feel that there is no time to enjoy things anymore.

Slower can also be a good thing if it benefits your end user in some way.

Slower can mean more relaxing, refreshing, rejuvenating, calming, reenergizing, and so on.

There are certain products and services that have advantages for being slower. Here are a few of them:

- PANASONIC EP 3007 (Panasonic's most advanced massage chair)
- SUBWAY Sandwiches (slower fast food, healthier)
- SLOW Beauty Salons (take it slow, get prettier)
- ORGANIC Products (produced slower, yet higher health benefit)
- STARBUCKS Coffee shops (built a whole industry around taking it slow, enjoying music and meeting friends while enjoying coffee)
- Cruises (slower travel while enjoying the scenery)
- SLOWFOOD.com (organization that supports healthier living)
- SLOW Fe Iron (iron slowly releases itself in the stomach)
- THE ORIENT EXPRESS A slow and scenic train trip.

How could you make YOUR product or service SLOWER? Write down your ideas: _____

176

Inno3: Bigness

BIGGER is better! (or so they say).

From BIGGER cars to BIGGER dishes to BIGGER people. Many things are getting BIGGER and BIGGER and BIGGER.

The US is probably the leading country for BIGGER. I've always admired how easy it comes to many Americans to think BIG.

BIGGER gives people a feeling that they've gotten MORE, that they've gotten something BETTER.

Creating BIGGER products and services can therefore lead to bigger revenues for companies.

Here are a number of bigness innovations which we now enjoy:

- AIRBUS A380 (World's largest passenger airplane can hold 2,022 passengers with 853 1st Class seats)

- Stretch limousines (world's longest is 100 feet long, created by Jay Ohrberg of Burbank California; includes Jacuzzi, sundeck, helipad, swimming pool, etc.)

- CONFERENCES (education moved from small classes of 20 to 20,000+ people attending a single conference)

- PANASONIC 3D TV (world's largest 3D TV at 152 inches)

- THE DUBAI MALL (world's largest shopping mall with 1.12 square kilometers and more than1,200 stores)

- THE BURJ KHALIFA - at 828m this tower in Dubai is the tallest building in the world

How could you make YOUR product or service BIGGER? Write down your ideas: _____

177

Inno4: Smallness

Just as many things are getting bigger, many are also going the other way. They are getting a lot smaller.

Smaller means handier, thinner, shorter or shrinking of a product or service.

Fitting an elephant through a door is hard. Some products and services just need to get smaller and smaller for us to have an advantage.

- MODU™ MOBILE (one of the world's smallest cell phones)

- Smaller TVs (nowadays lots of TVs are included in cell phones in Asia; here in South Korea almost everyone watches TV on their cell phones)

- APPLE iPod nano (do I need to say more?)

- SMART Car (one of the smallest cars created by Daimler AG)

- ASUS Eee PC (small notebook for a small price, changed the way we use notebooks and also its pricing)

- SMALLER apartments & offices (especially in Metropolitan cities where space matters; here in Seoul, South Korea you can find an office which is only 18 square meters starting from $500 upwards per month)

- CELL PHONE HANGERS (in Asia people hang teddy bears, mini-cosmetics (e.g. lip gloss), mini bus cards, mini mirrors, mini USB sticks, mini battery chargers, and even mini flashlights on their phones)

How could you make YOUR product or service SMALLER? Write down your ideas: _____

Inno5: Attractiveness

Key question: How can I make my product or service more attractive?

How is 'attractiveness' an innovation strategy?

Imagine you had the choice of picking one of two products. Product A has perfect technology. Product B has perfect technology PLUS gorgeous design.

Which one would you choose?

If you're like most people, you would of course choose product B.

That's the reason why beauty is a major innovation strategy. Houses are becoming more beautiful, so are cars, as are many other things around us.

Phillippe Starck, the world famous designer, even went so far as to make the humble toilet brush attractive.

This strategy can be especially big for industries who do not use it yet (e.g. like the computer industry did 20 years ago; now attractiveness is a major part of marketing a computer).

- ALL Apple Products (iPod, iPad, iMac, etc.)
- BANG & OLUFSON (the masters of sound are also the masters of attractiveness)
- Gourmet Food & Gourmet Food Restaurants (pretty looking food and even prettier looking plate design)
- TESLA Roadster (most attractive hybrid car built yet)
- HOWCAST.com (how-to website; more attractive than other websites because explains how-to information in fun, step-by-step, easy-to-watch and very high quality videos)

How could you make YOUR product or service MORE ATTRACTIVE? Write down your ideas: _____

179

Inno6: Ugliness

"Beauty is in the eye of the beholder", or so goes the famous saying.

Well, it goes beyond that too because: Ugly is the new beautiful.

Oddly enough many products seem to become more attractive as they get uglier. Some even have the purpose of being ugly to create beauty.

The ugliness strategy is about all innovations that go against the trend of the standard attractive innovations.

The funny thing is that after some while these ugly innovations are often considered very attractive as well.

Of course, people don't buy products that are ugly, but they buy them because they meet a certain emotional need with their ugliness (more on this in Step 4).

Let's have a look at a couple of ugly products or services that have succeeded big time:

- HONDA ZOOMER (naked, uglier motorbike)
- UGLY JEANS (Have you seen any "non-dirty" jeans lately?)
- MUD MASKS (dirt for beauty; literally)
- KICK SCOOTERS (ugly & slow, yet lots of people buy it and love it)
- MOBAGANDA.com (website for sending online invitations for events to your friends; much simpler and uglier than competitors like evite.com)
- THE YOUDOO DOLL (ugliest doll ever – no color, no face, no clothes, only the shape of a body made with white cloth – people can personalize it by drawing their friend's or enemy's faces on the doll).

How could you make YOUR product or service UGGLIER? Write down your ideas: _____

Inno7: Strength

Key question: How can I make my product or service stronger?

"An Indian feels no pain." Were the words of my dad said to me after I broke my arm when I was young. (The phrase is the common German expression for enduring pain.)

And yes, strength is attractive. Strength in products and services as well as in people.

The Strength Strategy is about products and services going to the extreme. They become so strong one way or another that they're either almost painful or indestructible.

- EARTHQUAKE ENGINEERING (engineers buildings that keep standing even after strong earthquakes used for example in the Taipei 101 skyscraper)

- HUMMER (one of the strongest SUVs built)

- ESPRESSO (stronger coffee)

- KOREAN BUL-DALK (probably the world's spiciest chicken)

- SPORTS MASSAGES (stronger massages)

- PURCHADE (sunscreen for plants to make them more sun resistant)

- STRONG WATCHES (from water-resistant watches to a watch that can withstand being driven over by a tank)

- STRONG UMBRELLA (the world's strongest umbrella can be stood on, or used to cut fruit, kill people (if needed) and still keeps you from getting wet; www.real-self-defense.com)

How could you make YOUR product or service STRONGER? Write down your ideas: _____

Inno8: Softness

Some innovations are softer than others.

Softer stands also for weaker, less and lighter.

Even though certain things need to become stronger and stronger, others need to become softer for other reasons like security or better feeling or taste, and so on.

- BEVERAGES (e.g. Café Latte = Coffee + Milk = Softer Coffee; Cocktails = liquor softened with sweet taste; Soft drinks 'light' versions like Diet Coke)

- J&J BABY SHAMPOO (softer shampoo for babies)

- BABY FOOD

- K2 Inline Skates (Soft boot inline skates, also used for snowboards)

- AIRBAG (softer for security)

- SOFT CONTACT LENSES (contact lenses that are softer for added comfort)

How could you make YOUR product or service SOFTER? Write down your ideas: _____

182

Inno9: Addition

Sometimes adding something small to a product can make a huge difference. Also, sometimes the add-on itself can be a great innovation.

Adding something small (or big) to your product or service can make a huge difference.

- CELL PHONE ADD-ONS (e.g. added TV, mp3, internet service, safety covers etc.)

- NINTENDO WII FIT (Add-on to the Nintendo Wii to get fit while having fun)

- FAST FOOD Sets (Burger + fried + coke + cheese cake + cheese sticks + ice-cream + salad + egg tart + chips)

- CAFÉ LATTE ADD-ONS (added to lattes: green tea, caramel, vanilla, honey, cinnamon, chocolate (Mocha), black tea, etc.)

- iHOME SPEAKERS (speakers made exclusively for the iPod; a whole new industry created around one little mp3 player)

- GOOGLE ADS (added advertisements that made up 99% of Google's revenues in 2008)

- COFFEE SLEEVE (invention that stops you from burning your fingers while enjoying your coffee; invented and patented by Jay Sorenson in 1993produced per year)

How could you ADD to YOUR product or service? Write down your ideas: _____

183

Inno10: Subtraction

In mathematical terms $2 - 1 = 1$.

When it comes to innovation though $2 - 1 = 3$.

Why? Because many innovations are created by subtracting something.

If you've ever had braces, you know how great it feels when they're finally gone. Many products out there run around with unnecessary braces.

Once you take the braces away, a great innovation is born. Here are some of them:

- HYBRID CARS (car MINUS gasoline)
- AMAZON KINDLE (what if we took away all books? Amazon's bestselling product as of 2010)
- CHEAP FLIGHTS (cheaper flights with less service = no food, smaller seats, etc. for a lower price, provided by Jet Blue, easyJet, etc.)
- TOUCHSCREEN PHONES (cell phones MINUS physical keyboard)
- DOUGHNUT PLANT (donuts MINUS eggs)
- MORE AFFORDABLE LUXURY CARS (luxury car MINUS size/performance, e.g. BMW 1 series, Mercedes A-Class, Audi A1, etc.)
- SKIM MILK (milk MINIUS fat)
- GOOGLE DOCS (Document program MINUS software package with CD and MINUS price, it's for free).
- DECAF (coffee MINUS the caffeine)

How could you SUBTRACT from YOUR product or service? Write down your ideas: _____

Inno11: Simplicity

Complex and difficult are as outdated as outhouses.

We live in a complex world, yes. And that's why all human beings crave simplicity.

Time is another factor. We all want to save as much of it as we can.

To achieve this, products have become simpler to use. Simplicity can significantly increase your chances of creating a winning innovation.

- GOOGLE (simplified browsing)

- PAYPAL.com (simplified payment method)

- CAR NAVIGATION SYSTEMS (simplified way to get to your destination)

- 24-Hour ATMs (simplified way to get money anytime)

- FLIP MINO (simplified video camera)

- HOME DELIVERY (simpler way of getting your food)

- ON-THE-GO PHONE CHARGER (easier method to recharge your cell phone while you're out and your battery is running out)

How could you SIMPLIFY YOUR product or service? Write down your ideas: _____

185

Inno12: Opposite Sex

Key question: How can I make my product or service for the opposite sex?

Why don't we create this for the opposite sex?

Scottish men started the trend by wearing skirts. Just kidding! Nowadays it looks like many products and services intended for women are beginning to focus on men and vice versa.

Products and services originally used only by men are now being created for women, whilst products and services originally used only by women are now being targeted at men.

Also unisex products, or products designed for both men and women, are now more and more available.

The trend is not as new as you might think, and has brought in multiple innovations created for the opposite sex.

- DIOR HOMME (female fashion brand now for men, since 2001)

- MEN's VOGUE (Vogue used to target women only, but since 2008 is available for men too)

- LEG SHAVING (men's shaver used to remove women's leg hair)

- MAKEUP FOR MEN (from eyeliner to powder to skin lightening)

- "SECRET" DEODORANT (based on ABC News more than 5 million men admit using the deodorant regularly)

- WNBA (the women's version of the National Basketball Association wasn't formed until 1996)

How could you make YOUR product or service FOR THE OPPOSITE SEX? Write down your ideas: _____

Inno13: Exclusivity

Key question: How can I make my product or service more exclusive?

Exclusive products and services say: '"This is not for everyone!"

In the past exclusivity was only promoted through price (and still is), but nowadays exclusivity also has another dimension: expert products and services.

Have a look at the following 3 factors:

Price – exclusive to those who can afford it

Time – exclusively available for a short time only

Expertise – exclusively for experts and celebrities of this product or service

- DESIGNER BAGS (designer bags are NOT for everyone)
- WOOT.com (one product available per day and then never again)
- SPACE TOURISM ($20-35 million to fly out to space for civilians)
- SUPERCARS (cars for the rich, from Lamborghini to Porsche to Bentley)
- DISNEY VAULT (Disney's old classic cartoon movies are only available in the market for a short period of time. Afterward they are put in a "vault" for up to 10 years and aren't available in the meantime, e.g. you can buy 'Snow White' only for a short period then it's unavailable for several years)
- FACEBOOK FOR SPIES (only true spies from FBI, CIA, NSA can join; NOT a joke!; the real name is "A-Space")
- GOLD SUNDAE (World's most expensive dessert, available in New York for a whopping $25,000)

How could you make YOUR product or service EXCLUSIVE? Write down your ideas: _____

Inno14: Inclusivity

> **Key question: How can I make my product or service available to more people?**

Inclusivity is the opposite of exclusivity.

Exclusivity is taking something normal and making it special and available to only a small group of people.

Inclusivity is the exact opposite.

Inclusivity is taking something that is exclusive and making it available to the masses, which can – if done right – lead to bigger success than the exclusivity strategy.

- ZARA (world's no. 1 fashion company makes high brand design at low prices for the masses)

- RENT-A-DESIGNER-BAG (yes, you can rent a Louis Vuitton for $100 a month; e.g. www.frombagstoriches.com)

- RENT-A-SUPERCAR (now everyone can drive a Supercar from Lamborghini to Ferrari at www.clubsportiva.com starting from $3,500 to $11,500 annually for 12 to 45 driving days per year)

- SUPERSTAR EDUCATION (superstar education going public for lower prices)

- SKYPE.com (the phone for the whole world for free, or at a low rate)

- VIRTUAL COACHING (online coaching using a coaching system, pay $10 instead of $500 or more per month)

- Screen Golf (famous in South Korea, play golf in a small room with REAL golf clubs and a virtual golf course on the screen for a small fee)

How could you make YOUR product or service INCLUSIVE? Write down your ideas: _____

Inno15: Connection

We as human beings have a huge need to connect with others.

People are afraid to be alone. People have a deep need to meet others, share ideas with others, and generally be connected with others.

So it's no surprise that many of the world's great innovations of all time actually fall into this category.

- FACEBOOK (connecting to your friends and getting even more friends)

- DUO (Korea's no. 1 matchmaking service, connecting for love)

- MSN Messenger (connecting online with instant messaging)

- NETWORKING EVENTS (meeting new people often for business purposes)

- CRAIGSLIST (connecting people who need something with those who have it)

- ONLINE GAMES (connecting with other players from around the world)

- TWITTER.com (instant messaging to be shared with as many people as want to hear from you)

- COWORKING a way of working that involves sharing a workspace with other workers that don't work for the same company as yourself, usually freelancers or independent contractors who don't want to work from home or a coffee shop.

How could you make YOUR product or service MORE CONNECTING? Write down your ideas: _____

Inno16: Personalization

Key question: How can I make my product or service more personalized?

Don't you hate getting mass printed cards for Christmas? Don't you love the ones that are written by hand?

People like things which have been personalized. They like feeling special. Also, they like creating things THEIR own way.

Tailors have always lived by this principle. They create a suit exactly the way you want it, that fits your body perfectly The world's best tailors consider every little detail of your body to create the perfect suit for you.

Just like good tailors, many innovative products and services focus on personalizing.

- PERSONALIZED MEDICINE (receive medicine perfectly tailored to your body type, especially famous here in South Korea from oriental doctors)

- BLOGGING (share your thoughts, on your own terms)

- YOUTUBE.com (create your own, personalized online TV)

- COLD STONE Ice Cream (create your personalized ice cream)

- TAILORED SHIRTS & SUITS (doesn't get more personalized than this. Nowadays anyone can get tailored clothes for affordable prices, e.g. mytailor.com)

- PERSONALIZED GIFTS (personalized promotional gifts for business partners are now easier and cheaper than ever)

How could you make YOUR product or service MORE PERSONALIZED? Write down your ideas: _____

Inno17: Correction

Key question: How can I make my product or service mistake-correcting?

Making mistakes is part of life. We all make them, and sometimes they just happen to us.

When you break your arm, you go to the hospital, and they fix it for you.

If your product can in some way correct mistakes that many people make and correct them quickly and easily, chances are high that you have a winning service or product.

- APPLE TIME MACHINE (a program that backs up all your files in real time automatically; no worries about losing files anymore)

- BIC Whiteout (correcting mistakes without having to rewrite or reprint)

- Program Spell Check (correcting any spelling mistakes you might make)

- ANTI-AGING PRODUCTS (stop looking older and start looking younger)

- SKIN WHITENING PRODUCTS (famous skin care products available in Asia where people want their skin to be whiter, available from all big skincare brands)

- PHARMACEUTICALS (e.g. Aspirin, good-bye headaches)

- ANTI-VIRUS PROGRAMS (correcting or preventing all of the computer viruses you've let into your system)

- SOLUTO - a software program that speeds up your computer's booting time by delaying the startup of resource hogging programs.

How could you make YOUR product or service MISTAKE-CORRECTING? Write down your ideas: _____

191

Inno18: Mobility

Key question: How can I make my product or service mobile?

Are you mobile yet?

Everything is becoming more mobile (and happily smaller too, so our arms don't hurt from too much carrying).

I remember when I was a young boy, I always had to carry heavy shopping bags for my grandmother. Nowadays, she simply orders what she wants over the phone for a few euros extra.

Mobility rocks!

- MP3 PLAYERS (10,000 songs in your pocket)

- RETAIL (mobile) DNA TEST (available from 23andMe for only $399; mobile way to figure out your predisposition for lots of traits ranging from baldness to blindness)

- AMAZON KINDLE (want to be able to carry your 1,000 book library with you? Amazon Kindle makes that possible)

- MOBILE GAMES (e.g. Nintendo, Gameboy, PSl,etc.)

- ANDROID (Google's mobile operation system for cell phones)

- PUSH UP PRO (fitness equipment to bring when you're out of town)

- Mobile food vans, selling everything from hotdogs to Korean BBQ tacos.

How could you make YOUR product or service MOBILE? Write down your ideas: _____

Innovation into Action

Take your product or service and run it through the Inno18. See what new ideas you can come up with for your product or service. Also make a note of how long it takes you to come up with the ideas using the Inno18.

1. Faster? _____

2. Slower? _____

3. BIGGER? _____

4. Smaller? _____

5. Attractive? _____

6. Uglier? _____

7. Stronger? _____

8. Softer? _____

9. Add-on? _____

10. Subtract? _____

11. Simplified? _____

12. Opposite sex? _____

13. Exclusive? _____

14. Inclusive? _____

15. Connecting? _____

16. Personalized? _____

17. Correcting? _____

18. Mobile? _____

Step 3

InnoCreation

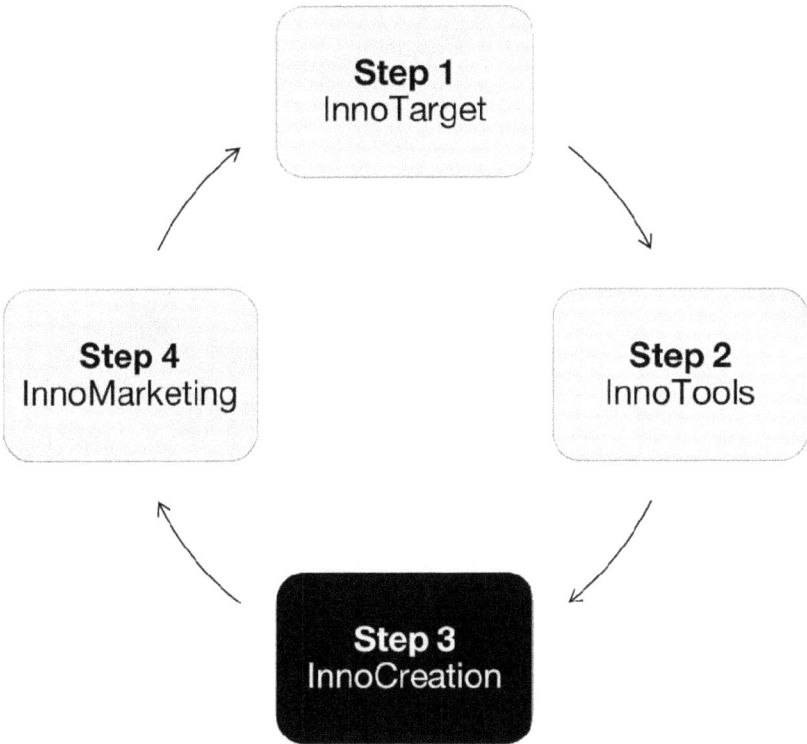

Step 1
InnoTarget

Step 2
InnoTools

Step 3
InnoCreation

Step 4
InnoMarketing

Why **Step 3:** InnoCreation?!

From InnoTools to InnoCreation

In Step 2: InnoTools you learned how to find lots of possible ideas and solutions to the problems and unmet needs that you defined in step 1. You should now have picked your best ideas and be ready to implement them.

In Step 3: InnoCreation you will turn your ideas into either a TANGIBLE product or service. This is the stage where your ideas become REAL.

The Problem in a Nutshell

Most people have never created anything.

And starting to create without a proven system can be a waste of time and money.

Many first time innovators fail to successfully turn their ideas into a product or service because they don't know how manage their resources. Even those who have already had experience creating products or services do so by wasting too many resources.

The Purpose of InnoCreation

The purpose of InnoCreation is to give you a step-by-step system to create a great product or service that is ready to be launched into the market.

You will learn the 6-step system used by most great innovators around the globe, and how to easily apply it.

Using this system will enable you to create products or services faster and (most importantly) with a higher chance of success.

When to Use InnoCreation

AFTER you've come up with tangible ideas in step 2.

Get ready to CREATE your product or service!

Draw Your Vision!

The first step to take when <u>creating</u> your product or service (after brainstorming all your ideas that is) is to draw your vision. And when I say draw, I mean draw.

Drawing aligns us with our EMOTIONAL side.

And your vision should evoke emotions in you: it needs to get you excited, or inspired or give you a sense of fulfillment.

The best feeling you can get about your vision is that it will change the world in some good, practical way and add lots of value to future users or clients.

Warren Buffet is famous for NOT investing in any company whose products or services he can't draw. He only buys stocks in the businesses whose products or services he fully understands and can easily sketch out on a piece of paper.

The first thing to do once you're done brainstorming (or often done during the brainstorming session itself) is to draw your vision.

Not the details. Not the next steps. But the end result. And that should include the people who will use your products or services.

What do you want the final product or service to look like? What is the end result?

I personally like to come up with a vision that reflects the final product or service as closely as possible. And the best way to express it is to actually draw the end result you would like to achieve using pen and paper. Don't forget to put it up on the wall afterwards so you can see your vision in front of you at all times.

The purpose of drawing is to make things visual. Chances are that if you can draw it, you can create it.

> # If you can draw it, chances are high you can create it.

Creators of great movies (directors, producers) often have a similar vision in their minds about the result of their movies. They see people fighting over tickets to watch their movies.

When Bill Gates envisioned 'a personal computer in every household in America', he not only envision the computer but also people using them sitting at their desks in their homes.

When Starbucks founder Howard Schultz envisioned the ultimate coffee experience, he saw a coffee shop where people could relax, meet with their friends or clients, or even finish off the slides for their big presentation to a client.

© YOONIQUE

The point is to try to imagine how happy your users will be with your new product or service innovation.

Remember: The reason you're creating the product or service should relate to them. Next comes the product or service itself.

Again in Step 1: InnoTarget, you needed your business, product or service to be determined by your users' list of needs and problems.

Next in Step 2: InnoTools, you had to come up with lots of solutions to the problems you'd identified.

Now, in this step, you need to put all the solutions together into one exciting vision from which you can create your product or service.

Without finding the problems and needs first and then finding possible solutions, it will be hard to create the vision and even harder to create an innovative product or service.

Great innovators have a vision for their product or service. Great innovators make their vision emotional, vivid and base it on the needs of their end users.

Innovation into Action

Draw your vision here:

Idea Organization

"Somewhere there is a map of how it can be done."

Ben Stein

After you have a clear vision that inspires you, you want to organize the parts you need to create to make that vision happen.

One of the best ways to organize your next detailed steps is to create a MIND MAP.

In many companies mind maps are standard. In some companies in Europe, you even have to be a master of mind maps to get into a managerial position.

Mind maps came into popular use through the work of Tony Buzan, bestselling author of Minds Maps. The concept of Mind maps, however, has been in use for hundreds of years as a way of organizing ideas.

Mind maps are of particular benefit because unlike lists, they are organized in a more friendly way for our brains.

It has even been said that mind maps closely mirror the brain's topology. Which is true, when you consider the neuron-associations in your mind that very much look like a jungle.

Here's a sample mind map (it's a simplified version of the original I used when creating this book):

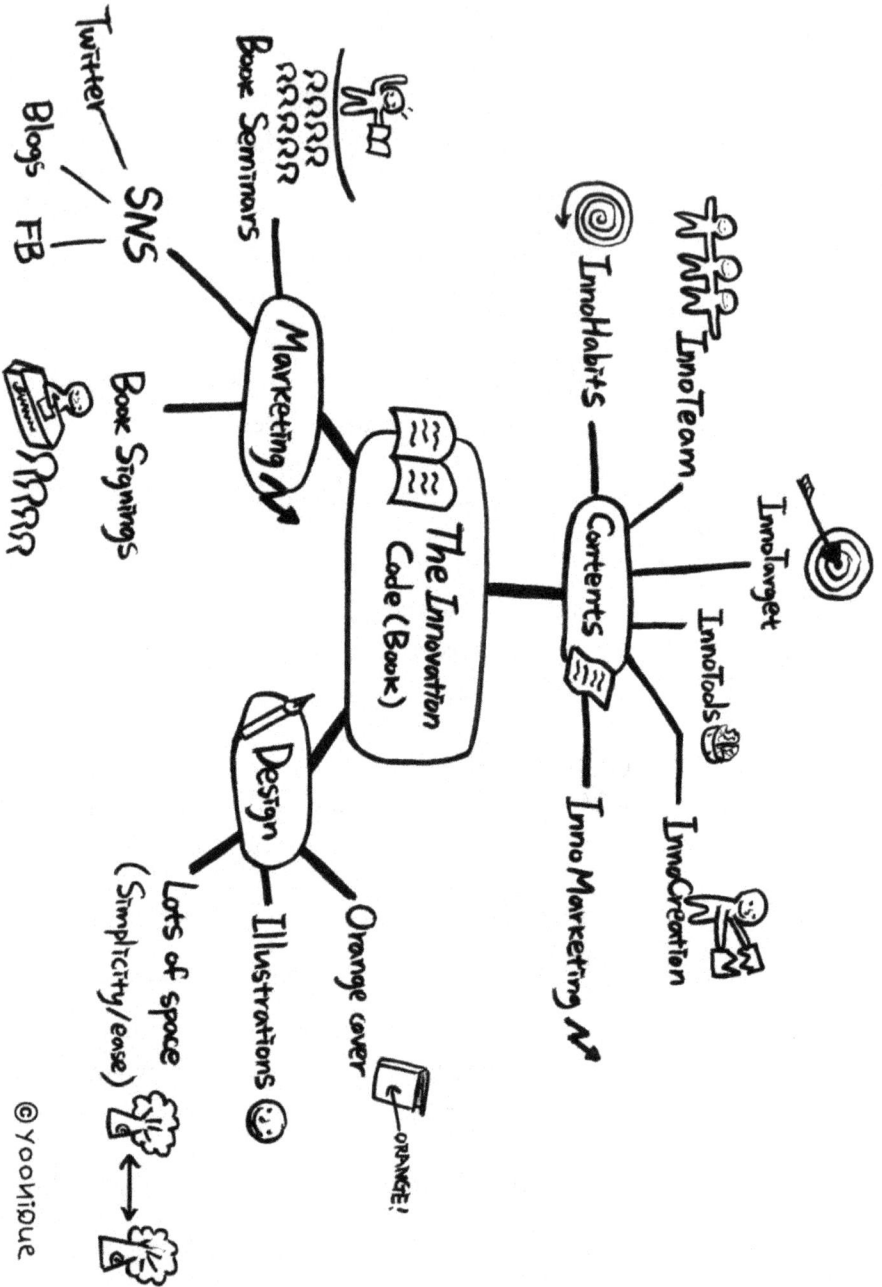

The Innovation Code (Book)

Marketing
- Book Seminars
- SNS
  - Twitter
  - Blogs
  - FB
- Book Signings

Contents
- InnoHabits
- InnoTeam
- InnoTarget
- InnoTools
- InnoCreation
- InnoMarketing

Design
- Orange cover — ORANGE!
- Illustrations ☺
- Lots of space (simplicity/ease)

© yoonique

204

Unlike what many people will tell you, I do NOT recommend using mind maps for brainstorming.

The reason is that they don't give you a framework to work with, like ABC Brainstorming or The Inno18 do.

You start from blank which, as I mentioned before, actually makes it harder to brainstorm.

BUT, mind maps are probably one of the best ways to organize information and remember it easily.

When using mind maps, you should keep the following 4 rules in mind:

1. Center it

Write the topic in the center of the page. Write it in bigger letters than the rest of your mind map. All other details will stem from your main topic and will radiate out from the center of the page, so make sure your main topic stands out before adding anything else.

2. Key words only

Write your ideas down as key words only. Key words help your brain make the connections. There is no need to write down whole phrases.

Choose key words that remind you of the entire idea. This way you can order your ideas easier, gain clarity faster and have the ability to see connections between ideas quicker.

Any bigger related ideas to your main topic can be structured as sub-ideas next to the topic using small arms.

3. Colors

Use many colors to stimulate your right brain and increase your retention of ideas.

4. Draw

Last, but not least, draw as many ideas as possible. Drawing will also stimulate your right brain and increase your retention of ideas. It will help you get more of your creative juices flowing and facilitate new ideas too.

Creating mind maps will most likely be very enjoyable for you. Many of our seminar participants have reported that creating mind maps feels easy and fun.

I've used mind maps for organizing the creation of many products and services I've created, from TV shows to books and even to companies. In fact, this book started out as a mind map, as you saw in the sample mind map above.

Of course, your mind map can be more detailed than the one above. Some companies use an entire wall just to mind map one project.

Some famous examples of companies using mind mapping:

BOEING once saved over $11 million using a mind map. They changed their Boeing Aircraft Engineering Manual into a 25-foot long Mind Map. That way a team of 100 senior aeronautical engineers was able to learn in a few weeks, what used to take a few years.

EDS and Nabisco used Mind Maps for a group of 120 senior managers in one of their study programs. Participants were able to process the equivalent of 4-6 days of training in a one-day study session.

So keep in mind that when you create an overview of all the things necessary to make your vision a reality, it's important to include all the details that are needed to make that possible. And again, those details can best be organized using mind maps, because they will give you a big picture of your project.

Great innovators use mind maps to organize their ideas. They create mind maps using the 4 rules and in a way that helps them come up with even more ideas.

Innovation into Action

Create your mind map here (include as many details as possible). Start by writing the current name of the new product or service you want to create in the center and then take it from there.

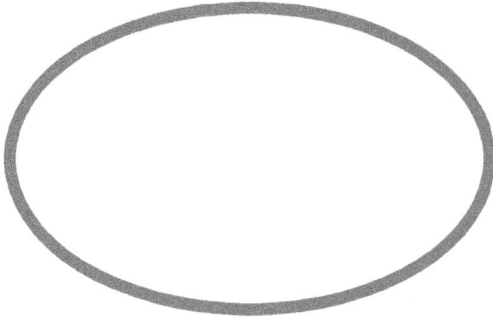

Product Prototyping

What is prototyping?

Simply put, a prototype is a 3D version of your vision.

This is the step where you take your ideas and vision and give them shape and form.

So you can see your product in front of your eyes.

So you can touch it.

So you can finally feel like it's becoming a reality.

Product prototyping can be one of the most enjoyable exercises because you can SEE your vision and FEEL it as well.

Product prototyping has the following benefits:

1. You can test if your idea works in reality.

2. You can better see the reactions of future users or clients.

3. You can be more confident in your idea.

Prototyping is the start to making your ideas TANGIBLE.

When creating a prototype you want to keep in mind that you should start with a LOW COST version first.

209

The reason for this is simple. At the beginning create the lowest-cost, easiest-to-break version, because chances are high that you will break it or at the very least want to revise it. At this stage you're still ironing out all the kinks or imperfections that weren't obvious to you until you had a tangible product in hand.

Later on as you move closer to the final product, you can invest in more advanced prototypes.

A mistake that almost all first-time prototype creators make is to invest too much money in their first prototype.

All experienced prototype creators will tell you that that's just silly.

Why invest so much in an as-yet-unproven product?

I once spent all my money on a product I believed in, only to find that I'd spent my money at the wrong time. I put my idea straight into production without testing it first. When the product failed after some testing so too did the whole project. Stupid? Sure! Good lesson? Definitely! Don't make the same mistake. Learn from mine.

So, when creating your product prototype take it step-by-step.

Low-cost ways to start creating your prototypes include using LEGO, cardboard, clay, paper, glue, tape, wood, staples, etc. The key here is LOW COST.

Choose from the above list to suit the product you're creating. Play around with it, and find out what's right for your particular needs.

Also, if you work in a FORTUNE 500 company and you have a big budget, you'll want to start with a simple low cost version first. Why waste your company's money?

If you're creating a bigger product, you might want to start out with a miniature version first and master it before moving on to a full-scale (and more expensive) prototype.

Later on you can get the real material for the final version and play around with it until you're satisfied and your vision has turned into reality.

Also, you'll want to think outside the box sometimes and play around with new materials.

For example, when Nike came up with its first superior sports shoe sole, it happened in some ways by accident. Read for yourself:

"The company's first self-designed product was based on Bowerman's "waffle" design. After the University of Oregon resurfaced the track at Hayward Field, Bowerman began experimenting with different potential outsoles that would grip the new urethane track more effectively. His efforts were rewarded one Sunday morning when he poured liquid urethane into his wife's waffle iron. Bowerman developed and refined the so-called 'waffle' sole which would evolve into the now-iconic Waffle Trainer in 1974." - Wikipedia

Was the new sole created through well planned thinking, or was it achieved by chance?

I think it's a little bit of both.

Sometimes you figure out the best way that works for your new product or service by thinking the idea through in step 2 (Innovation Tools) and sometimes in step 3 (Innovation Creation). Either way, what matters is the end result.

By the way, don't worry if you're not the perfect product prototyper. Remember: If you don't have the skill or the right person on your team, you can always find someone who does.

You can create the first rough looking version and then bring it to a professional. They should be able to take it to the next level (if not you've not found the right person).

Sometimes you need an engineer, sometimes a machinist, sometimes a CAD specialist, sometimes a rapid prototyping expert.

Ideally you have the person you need working in your company.

If not, the best ways to find product prototyping companies and experts is either online or in your network. So far I've found all the help I needed by asking the people around me to recommend someone they know.

If your network cannot bring you the right person or company, you need to find them online. Go to www.alibaba.com and type in "Product Prototype". You will be able to find companies specializing in product prototyping from more than 20 different countries.

Great Innovators prototype their products. They create prototypes to identify problems (which they later solve), to gain more ideas and insights, and to have a physical manifestation of their ideas.

Innovation into Action

Do your product prototyping and record your insights here:

_____

_____

_____

_____

_____

Service Prototyping

First off - what are service innovations?

When most people think of innovation, they only think of products and NOT services. But products are only half the story.

Not only do service innovations exist, they offer as much if not more value than product innovations.

From banking industry innovations to health service innovations to professional service innovations, it's all there and new innovations keep coming up in all industries every single year.

So just as with product innovations, before launching your services, you should test them as well.

In terms of service what always matters is what you DO and HOW you do it.

So the best way to prototype a new service innovation is by ROLE-PLAYING out the whole scenario.

HOW will you deliver your service?

Often what you do BEFORE you offer your main service and AFTER you offer your main service is just as important as the main service itself, in some cases even more important.

For example, before trainers deliver workshops to clients they often need to do a needs analysis BEFORE the actual training. In some cases they need to meet with the participants in advance and interview them. All this helps the trainer deliver a near perfect service experience based on insight given before they even deliver the service.

After the workshop, trainers often need to write a workshop report and share the evaluation results they received from participants. It is also not uncommon to have a feedback session with the client to talk about what happened during the workshop.

The BEFORE and AFTER matters in the service industry!

Another example can be the service of flying.

BEFORE you enter an airplane, you have to drive to the airport and possibly park. You have to check in your luggage. You have to get your boarding pass. You have to go through security. You have to find the right gate for your flight. And in the meantime you probably want to do some shopping in the duty free section.

With this in mind, how do you feel about the BEFORE service of flying?

Let's face it. Most people would agree it's not the most enjoyable experience. Queuing up. Security check. Boarding the plane. Negotiating for space for your carry-on luggage in the overhead bins. These are all things that airlines and airport companies need to continue to improve on to make the flying experience a more pleasant one.

So, when prototyping a new type of service keep the before and after in mind.

The best way to create a killer service is by first ROLE-PLAYING the old process (to find mistakes), then mapping out the new improved service on paper, and then role-playing again with possible users.

You need to ROLE-PLAY!

Role-play the whole service experience.

Pretend YOU are the user and try it out. In between, as always look for problems, unpleasant things or little pains that might annoy your users.

In fact, role-playing is the ONLY way to create a great experience!

Why?

Because to understand the EXPERIENCE, you need to EXPERIENCE it.

Thinking about it won't do it. Sleeping on the problem won't do it. The only way to do it is to experience it.

Starbucks are masters at creating a service experience that works.

From the music (not too loud, not too low) to lighting (not to bright, not to dim) to the color and texture of the pictures on the wall and chairs you put your fanny on. They all blend in perfectly with Starbuck's overall strategy: Providing their users with a 2nd home.

Also, the people who work behind the counter at Starbucks are trained to meet the needs of their customers by making sure that every question they ask counts. Again, the perfect service experience created.

The coffee of course always tastes the same, you have thousands of beverage options and 4 size options (short, tall, grande, venti) and if you get a take-out cup, you get a coffee sleeve with it so you don't burn your fingers.

The Starbucks example sounds simple, doesn't it?

The Starbucks experience feels natural when we visit, doesn't it?

But is it really?

Or did the company invest years in perfecting their system to iron out any and all small problems or inconveniences and create the perfect experience for their customers?

Great Innovators prototype their services before bringing them to the market. They ROLE-PLAY their services. They EXPERIENCE their services themselves. They let REAL clients or users ROLE-PLAY their service prototype to get REAL feedback.

Innovation into Action

Conduct your service prototyping and record your insights here:

_____

_____

_____

_____

_____

Test, Test, Test

"I didn't fail the test, I just found 100 ways to do it wrong."

Benjamin Franklin

I don't think anyone has ever created a product or service without making numerous mistakes in the testing process.

Nothing I've created so far has ever been perfect on the first try.

You won't be able to achieve perfection on your first try either, so don't worry. Make more mistakes and learn along the way.

The secret to create and finish a marketable idea that works is to Test, Test, Test!

Test, test, test, test, test, test, test, test....

Testing really matters when creating your product or service. Not just the test on the product or service itself, but especially on the future users or clients who are supposed to buy it from you or your company.

Groups you can test your products on include:

- Focus Groups

- 1-on-1 tests with users

- Tests in real environment

- Tests on non-users

217

Also, different industries require different testing methods. Usually you need to meet certain standards. So for your own industry you need to research and check what these are (e.g. meeting hygiene standards if you're in the food & beverage industry).

© yoонique

But in general all innovators need to focus on the following 6 principles when creating their products or services to achieve great results:

1. Speed

How fast and how easy is it to produce the product or create the service? Speed matters especially when it comes to competitors. If you're not fast enough, you might miss the boat.

2. Simplicity

Is your product or service simple enough for your end users? If so, you have a winner. If not, you need to keep testing and working on it until it is easy enough for your ideal client to use your product or service. If it's not simple enough, someone else might create a simple enough version that will sink yours.

3. Usefulness

Is it really useful? If your product or service isn't useful enough, no one will buy it. Does it really meet a need or solve a problem? If not, you need to go back to Step 1: Innovation Target. Because, if it's not useful no one will buy it.

4. Affordability

Is your product or service affordable? You need to tackle this question from two angles: Is it affordable enough for the end user to buy? And also, does it make business sense for you to produce? Can you produce it at a good enough price that will entice your clients to buy but that allows you to make a profit? If it's not affordable for you, you might create value, but lose money. Conversely, if it's not affordable for them, they simply won't buy.

5. Legal Protection

Have you checked how you can legally protect your product or service from competitors? Do you need patents or trademarks to protect your intellectual property? If you create a great product or service you also need to protect it. If it's not protected you might have grown your own competition overnight.

6. Environment

Is the product, creation, application or delivery of your product or service environmentally-friendly? Creating products and services that care about the environment and help preserve it matter and are a must nowadays.

You can use the 6 principles above as a checklist when testing your product or service to make sure that you don't step into any sinkholes when you're so close to the finish line.

Great Innovators test, test, test. They use the 6 testing principles to make sure that their product or service really has the potential to become a winner.

Innovation into Action

Test your product based on the following 6 standards:

Speed - How fast and how easy is it to produce the product or create the service?

_____

Simplicity – Is your product or service simple enough for your end users?

_____

Usefulness – Is it really useful?

_____

Affordability – Is your product or service affordable? (for you AND the client)

_____

Legal Protection – Have you checked how you can legally protect your product or service from competitors?

_____

Environment Is the product, creation, application and delivery of your product or service environmentally-friendly?

_____

Create an Experience

"What we sell is the ability for a 43-year-old accountant to dress in black leather, ride through small towns, and have people be afraid of him."

Harley Davidson Executive

What is the ultimate product or service you can create?

One that creates an entire EXPERIENCE for the end user!

The ultimate measurement of EXPERIENCE of course is the EXPERIENCE SYSTEM. The system that makes sure you have the same great experience every single time you buy the product or service.

Creating and selling a great product is good.

Creating and selling a great service is good.

Creating and selling an EXPERIENCE is OUTSTANDING!!!

And OUTSTANDING is what will make your product or service a success.

Does Harley Davidson sell motorcycles? No! They sell the EXPERIENCE of being a bad-ass.

Does Emirate Airlines just help you get from A to B? No! They make you feel like a sheikh the whole way.

Does Samsung just sell cell phones? No! They sell the EXPERIENCE of having the coolest-looking-easy-to-use-fun-to-show-off-and-most-importantly-indestructable cell phones you can get.

Does BMW sell cars? No! They sell the EXPERIENCE of 'the ultimate driving machine' that gives you the feeling of being high-class yet sporty, comfortable yet luxurious all at the same time.

Does Google sell a search engine? Hell no! They sell the EXPERIENCE of YOU having the world at your fingertips (literally).

> ## Make your products or service an EXPERIENCE that your users will remember.

All great companies on the planet create EXPERIENCES and if you want to truly succeed you should turn your product or service into an EXPERIENCE too.

Is it tough to create an experience?

You bet it is!

That's why there are so few great companies out there.

I know firsthand how hard it is to create EXPERIENCES through my experience creating workshops for my business INFLUENCE7.

A workshop should really be an EXPERIENCE that helps people learn new skills, change behaviors or create a better perception of themselves.

Workshop creators and designers have one of the toughest jobs on the planet.

The best of us know that creating a great workshop is like creating 'Disneyland' for a group of people.

For each new workshop you need to re-consider everything: the workshop activities, the contents, the room setup from chairs to white board to light to plants (yes, plants!; for all kinds of reasons related to feng shui), to the cultural background of the audience, to corporate culture to typical behavior of the audience (trust me there are worlds apart between training doctors or engineers or marketing staff or the executive team) to the music you choose (based on each group's background). And the list goes on and on and on...

Is it fun? Yes! (for some crazy people like myself).

Is it tough? YES!

Trust me, all this includes lots of painful testing and practicing, yet once all these problems are cracked each workshop is a guaranteed winner.

An EXPERIENCE that delivers time after time after time.

Dull Car   Experience Car

When you intend to create an experience, focus on the following:

1. Know your end user inside-out

Again, it goes back to knowing your end users. Know what their preferences are. What they want. What they can't live without. What their biggest problems are. What their gripes are.

2. Ask yourself: Is my experience an ENTIRELY positive event?

At which parts of your experience does your end user experience some NEGATIVE emotions? Those are the things that – if solved – can make the biggest difference.

Annoyed with having to go to the bank during your lunch break? No problem! Internet banking saves you the hassle by allowing you to manage your account from the comfort of your own home, anytime of day or night.

Based on audience or cultural background the workshops my team and I create are either more high-energy and active or not (e.g. Indians prefer super-high energy, whereas Koreans need time at the beginning to warm up, but later – once they get to know you better – are willing to go for high energy experiences during training).

3. Test until all you hear is "WOW!"

A truly amazing product or service is created when the clients or users say WOW! and they get the results they want every single time.

Great Innovators set out to create EXPERIENCES. They intend their users to say 'WOW!'

Innovation into Action

What can you do to turn your product or service into a memorable EXPERIENCE? Which famous companies can you think of (both inside and outside of your industry) that create experiences for their end users, and how do they do it?

Company   How they create an experience

_____   _____

_____   _____

_____   _____

_____   _____

_____   _____

Fix Problems Until Finalized

LOVE problems!

Yes, you've read correctly: Love them!

Take problems as a godsend!

Better to find them out earlier than later.

It costs less money and time to fix problems in the early stages of a project when you have 10 prototypes versus when you have 100,000 finished products sitting in a warehouse waiting to get to market.

You should be in love with all problems you find along the way.

And as problems arise, you can go back to Brainstorming!

> ## Problems are your friends. In all parts of the innovative process problems are the key to creating your innovation.

Sometimes you come up with the perfect ideas and solutions for all possible problems during brainstorming and all you have to do is execute. It is the rare product or service that is perfect from the get go.

Sometimes (more often than not) you'll find lots of mistakes during the testing phase. If that's the case, and most of the time it is, you'll need to go back to brainstorming.

Be ready with your list of problems and start using the brainstorming techniques you learned earlier in this book until you come up with ideal solutions.

Again fixing problems means working together with your end users. Getting their feedback can be invaluable before creating the final product or service.

You don't want to discover more problems later (which tends to be more expensive for any type of innovator: from small-scale inventor to FORTUNE 500 innovation expert; either way you and your company lose).

Once you feel every single problem has been resolved to your satisfaction, your product or service should be done and be ready to 'go live'.

I'm often asked: "When do I know that I'm done?"

This is a tough question, because that depends on your level of perfectionism.

Should Microsoft have put MS 3.1 on hold until they finalized MS Windows 95?

Some people say yes, others say no.

Some companies prefer bringing products into the market faster (to get real feedback from lots of users) and then upgrade their products afterwards.

(One recent example is the Apple iPad, which I personally feel came out as a market tester to allow for further development.)

Some companies spend more time testing in labs.

So my answer is very simple: Based on your (and your company's) level of PERFECTIONISM, you need to decide for yourself.

Bringing out a product or service sooner often has the benefit of getting more feedback faster. And based on that you can decide to continue with it (if proven successful), or to let it go (if proven unsuccessful).

Bringing out your product or service later has the benefit of better quality (in some cases if you've tested with REAL end users) and of course has the downside that it takes longer to test the real success in the market place and get real feedback.

Hence, you'll need to choose YOUR level of perfectionism.

Great Innovators fix all problems until their product or service is finalized. They decide when it is finalized and ready for release according to their own level of perfectionism.

Innovation into Action

List some of the problems you've discovered and possible solutions to fix them.

Problems   **Possible Solutions**

_____   _____

_____   _____

_____   _____

_____   _____

_____   _____

_____   _____

_____   _____

Step 4
InnoMarketing

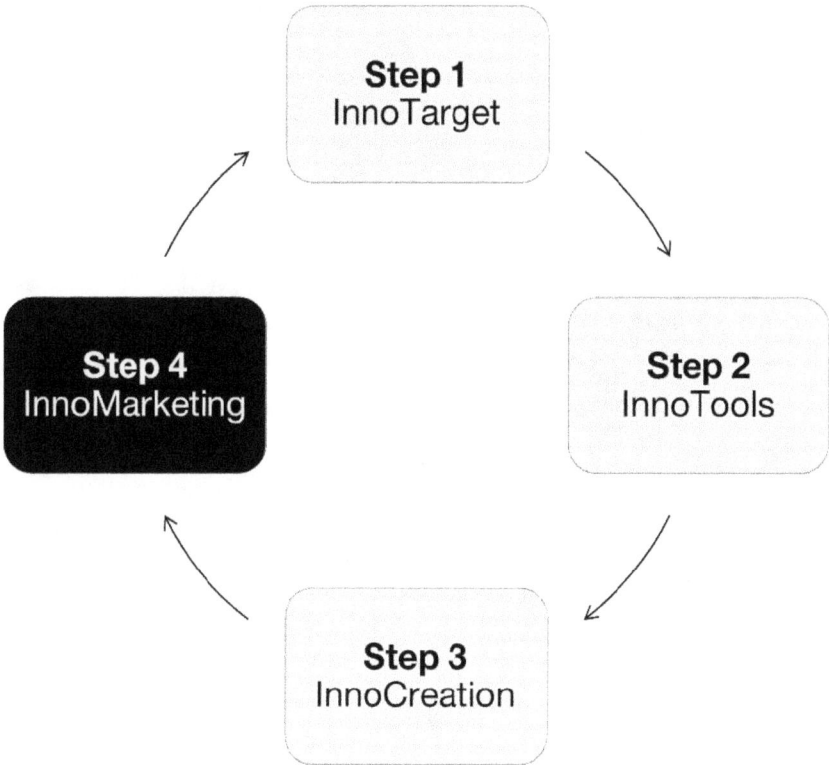

Why **Step 4:** InnoMarketing?!

From InnoCreation to InnoMarketing

In Step 3: InnoCreation you finalized your product or service and got it ready to be launched into the market.

In Step 4: InnoMarketing you will take your product or service and make it even MORE ATTRACTIVE for your ideal users through the use of proven marketing strategies.

The Problem in a Nutshell

Lots of products or services are great, yet perform poorly because of poor marketing.

If you have a great product or service but the world doesn't know about, how good is it?

The other problem is that most product or service creators have NO CLUE about marketing. They might have a winner on their hands but have no clue how to communicate its value to their end users.

The Purpose of InnoMarketing

The purpose of InnoMarketing is NOT to give you everything you need for marketing (that in itself would be a whole other book), but to give you the basics to marketing your product or service well in the market place.

You will learn how to create strong benefits, an attractive visual surface, a recognizable name and more, faster and smarter.

233

All these small things will ultimately add up and create the foundation for the BRAND strategy of your product or service.

When to Use InnoMarketing

Usually AFTER you create your final product, though I also suggest you to constantly consider the things in this chapter during all the other 3 steps. Thinking about the marketing during product or service creation can often lead to an even better product or service (I personally never create without keeping the contents of this chapter in mind).

Get ready to create your InnoMarketing!

The Importance of Marketing

"The fact is, everyone is in sales. Whatever area you work in, you do have clients and you do need to sell."

Jay Abraham, renowned marketing expert

Which phone is more famous? The LG Prada phone or the Apple iPhone?

You will no doubt say the iPhone.

And if you ask most people, which of the two was the first touch screen phone on the market, the answer will most likely be the same.

"The iPhone!"

Unfortunately (or fortunately for the iPhone) this is not true. The first touch screen phone on the market was in fact the LG Prada cell phone.

The LG Prada was first released in Korea in Christmas of 2006, whereas the iPhone only came out on June 29, 2007.

Yet, why do we think that the iPhone was the first?

Another example: Have you ever heard of a person called Leif Ericson? Chances are you haven't.

The last thing you would probably think is that Leif Ericson was the first European to set foot in what we now call America.

Surely, the first European to get to America was Christopher Columbus, right?

Sorry, but you're wrong!

235

Leif Ericson was the first European to do so, fully 500 years before Christopher Columbus.

Yet, if you asked 1,000 people around the world who discovered America, over 99% would probably say Christopher Columbus.

How is it that Christopher Columbus is regarded as being the first?

Both examples convey the same message: It is not about who is the first to create or discover something, it's the one who SHOWS the world their creation or discovery who will be remembered to be the first.

To put it simply: to get your product (or company) famous, you need to MARKET it to the world.

Marketing is at the heart of every product or service.

Hardly any product or service in the world gets famous, by virtue of its existence alone.

You need to let the world know what you have, and the best way to do that is to use strong marketing.

The iPhone won out over the LG Prada, because Apple made it their #1 marketing effort of 2007. Christopher Columbus got famous because he was sponsored by Queen Isabella I of Castile and because his voyages happened at an important time of economic competition between European countries.

The main thing to remember: ultimately marketing will either make or break your product or service.

Great quality will give you a shot at creating a winning innovation, but if your marketing cannot back it up, other companies will quickly take over your initial success.

So, make sure that you study marketing as much as you do creativity, and hone your marketing skills as much as you do the skills associated with your craft.

In the following chapter, I will share just a couple of marketing tips with you, but I also strongly suggest that you study some of the best marketing books you can find to master this skill.

Attractive Benefits

"Your premium brand had better be delivering something special, or it's not going to get the business."

Warren Buffett

"Why should I choose your product or service over anyone else's?"

That's the main question your product or service should answer.

Even more so, that is the question your marketing should answer.

To answer that question properly you need to highlight the benefits of your product or service.

So, let's have a look at how you can best do that.

Overall benefits

The best way to highlight the benefits of your product or service is, as we discussed earlier in this book, to solve clients' problems, pains and unmet needs.

Let's just say you want to buy a new product, your problem and benefit assessment might look like this:

Problem   Notebooks are too big & heavy.

Benefit   Our notebook is slim & light (it weighs only 1.7kg - Asus Computers).

Or if you want to become a superstar, it might look like this:

Problem   I'm a good singer, but I have no chance to get a deal with a record company.

Benefit   We give you a chance to prove yourself against thousands of competitors and millions of viewers from all over the world. If you succeed you get your record deal and support from us (American Idol).

So, this is one way to do it.

You could make a list of all the problems your product or service solves and of all the benefits it provides.

Strong benefits create a stronger product or service.

What are the benefits of your product or service that help solve your client's pains, problems or unmet needs?

Record at least 5 benefits of your product or service:

1. _____

2. _____

3. _____

4. _____

5. _____

USP (Unique Selling Proposition)

Another thing you'll want to do after you have your list of specific benefits is to create a Unique Selling Proposition (USP).

A USP is a single phrase that summarizes the main benefit of the product very clearly and is later used as a slogan in all marketing and advertising efforts.

Let's have a look at a couple of USPs that made products or services famous:

Youtube	Broadcast yourself.
Youdoo Doll	Love it. Hate it. Hug it. Hurt it. Play with it. Punish it.
Google Translate	Translate over 50 languages.
BMW X1	Joy is a life full of possibilities. (German: "Freude is voller Moeglichkeiten.")
Guinness Beer	Guinness refreshes your spirit. (US campaign)

What do you notice?

USPs usually have one or more of the following in common:

- Highly PRACTICAL (Translate over 50 languages / Broadcast...)

- EMOTIONAL (Joy is... / Love it. Hate it... / Guinness refreshes)

- YOU-focused (Broadcast yourself. / ...your spirit.)

Look up the USPS of some of your favorite products and services, and list 5 of them here:

_____

_____

_____

What's your main benefit in one phrase? The one that has the biggest impact? How would you describe it in one powerful USP? Start writing your initial ideas down here:

_____

_____

OFS Benefits

Another thing you want to consider is a formula which I call OFS benefits. OFS stands for: Opinions, Facts & Stories.

Opinions

Opinions are what you think about your product or service. Opinions are claims that are not backed up by facts. Here are a couple of opinions:

- "Our cell phone is the most gorgeous on the planet."

- "Our sandwiches have the lowest fat."

- "Our car is the fastest."

Facts

Facts on the other hand talk about specific numbers and details which make your products/services more believable to potential users/clients.

- "Our cell phone comes in 10 colors."

- "Our sandwiches have 30% less fat than all our competitors."

- "Our car goes from 0 to 100 in 5.7 seconds."

Stories/Examples

Even better than facts are real stories or examples. Think about it this way: Would you rather buy a product because you read about the facts or because you tested it and your friend said it was great?

Chances are your own testing and your friend telling you it's great will win out.

- "Our cell phone is used by Brad Pitt. If you use it, you can be as popular with your friends as Brad is."

- "One of our customers lost 20 pounds eating our sandwiches daily."

- "Our car has been tested by the world famous car TV show *Top Gear* and has been voted best in comparison to all other cars in its class."

The best marketing of any product is of course when there is a balance of OFS (Opinions, Facts, and Stories) in your marketing messages.

Which OFS do you need to add to your benefits? Which one do you need to work on the most?

What is one opinion, one fact and one story that highlights the benefits of your product or service in the most powerful way?

Opinion: _____

Fact: _____

Story: _____

One powerful example of how a company or product used a great story to sell more products comes from SUBWAY Sandwiches.

You might have heard of (or seen) Jared S. Fogle, now also known as the Subway Guy.

His story is very simple yet compelling: He lost 245 pounds eating mainly Subway sandwiches.

The company picked up the story, made him spokesperson, and since the story came out in 2000, Subway's sales have more than doubled to $8.2 billion.

It's amazing how much impact the RIGHT story can have!

Great Innovators point out the strong benefits of their product or service. Their benefits offer solutions to problems. Their main benefit is summarized in one phrase. They balance opinions, facts and stories when pointing out their benefits.

The 4 Emotional Benefit Factors

As we discussed earlier in Step 1: InnoTarget, people buy based on emotions and back up their purchasing decisions with logic later.

So, what are the strongest emotional triggers for people?

They can be summarized in four words: Money, Sex, Relationships and Health.

© yoonique

Money is a strong emotional need because it provides power, status, wealth, ability to show off (and feel superior), confidence and security.

Sex stands for all of the following: love, excitement, pleasure, intimacy, attraction and strength.

Relationships give a strong benefit because they combine belonging, family, friends, bonding, caring and support.

Health is about well-being, beauty, happiness, feeling invigorated, physical wellness, energy, and vitality.

Money	Sex	Relationships	Health
Power	Love	Belonging	Well-Being
Status	Excitement	Family	Beauty
Wealth	Pleasure	Friends	Happiness
Showing off	Intimacy	Bonding	Physical wellness
Confidence	Attraction	Caring	Energy
Security	Strength	Support	Vitality

If you want to try a fun exercise right now, try the following: pull out a magazine and flip through it. Look at all the advertising you can see.

Next, ask yourself: Which of the 4 emotional factors are they using for the advertisements you're looking at?

In some cases they use only one, but in most cases advertisers often use two or three of these emotional triggers simultaneously to get people attracted to their brands (and it doesn't matter what the product is - from cars to shampoo to TVs, and so on).

Of course, the 4 emotional triggers are not only limited to advertisements. You can use them for anything from the visuals you use on your packaging, to articles you write about your product or service for a magazine (and writing about the emotional trigger), to any of the other marketing materials you use.

Car companies like BMW or Mercedes always use MONEY as their main emotional trigger. For target users who are singles they often add SEX to the mix.

For larger cars they focus on families and in so doing add RELATIONSHIPS to their marketing mix. And in few cases they highlight the car's security, in which case they focus on the HEALTH factor.

When you watch APPLE advertisements and commercials, you will quickly realize that they use MONEY as their main emotional trigger. They also often use RELATIONSHIPS as their trigger (the relationship in their commercials between the two people called 'PC' and 'Mac').

Alcoholic beverages around the world are sold mainly through one of two triggers: SEX or RELATIONSHIPS. In a cases where it's a premium alcohol being marketed, alcohol companies add MONEY to their emotional mix.

Which emotional triggers can best work for your product or service to grab the interest of your target user?

Great Innovators are clear on which emotional triggers to use. Great innovators are truly benefit-focused.

Innovation into Action

Which of the 4 emotional benefit factors is/are best to market your product or service? After choosing, describe how you can best include the factor(s) in your marketing efforts.

Money　　　**Sex**　　　**Relationships**　　　**Health**

_____

_____

_____

Attractive Naming

Naming a product is like naming a baby.

There is truly a hair's-breadth of difference between the two. If you give your child a silly name, your child will be made fun of at school. If you give your product a silly name, it will be made fun of in the market place.

> Naming your product is like naming your child. If you fail other kids will make fun of it.

Either way a silly name can prevent a product or service from reaching its full market potential.

On the other hand a great name can propel and increase the chances of your product or service's success in the market place.

When giving your product a name, you want to follow my naming guideline acronym GUMSEL which stands for:

G lobal

U nique

M emorable

S hort

E asy-to-Use

L egal

1. Global

The first guideline to follow is to make sure that the name you choose is globally usable, or choose a different name for each country.

Too many market entry failures have happened, because of poor name selection.

Consider the following examples.

When the Mazda *Laputa* entered the Spanish speaking markets, the scandal was huge. Why? *La puta* means 'prostitute' in Spanish. Would you want to drive around in a 'prostitute'?

Another fun car example is the Chevy Nova when it was introduced to South America. In Spanish *no va* means 'won't go'. Would you buy a car that 'won't go'?

When choosing a brand name, check for global usability in the markets you wish to enter.

2. Unique

Second, you want to make your name unique, but in a good way.

Great unique examples of names are 'Krispy Kreme' or the 'Yoo-doo Doll' that I mentioned earlier in the book.

They are truly unique and stand out.

3. Memorable

Next you want to make sure that your name is memorable.

An old Samsung cell phone is called the *T229*. How memorable is that? Hardly, if at all.

Imagine running to your friend and saying 'Hey the new *T229* is awesome!' I doesn't matter if you convince him to buy it or not, because by the time he gets to the store, he will already have forgotten the name.

That was several years ago when the standard that most mobile phone companies would follow was to create silly alphanumeric names that nobody could remember.

Thankfully things have changed.

Samsung's latest phone called *Impression* not only makes a real impression, but is also extremely easy to remember.

Is your product's name memorable?

4. Short

In general, shorter names are easier remembered than longer ones.

Going back to the example of naming your child, many people get long names when they're born. What do most people with long names do? They shorten them!

For example, my full name is Benjamin, but no one except my mother ever calls me that. I am widely known as Ben.

Let's have a look at a product example:

Which name do you prefer:

a. Microsoft Windows Vista Ultimate UPGRADE Limited Numbered Signature Edition

b. Apple Mac OS X

Of course, you would choose the second one.

How about the name of your product and service: is it short enough to be remembered?

5. Easy to Use

This one goes hand in hand with being memorable.

The test for ease of use is whether people can easily use the name of your product or service in everyday conversation.

There's a mini notebook from Samsung called the *NP-N120*.

If your friend called you on the phone asking you what you're doing would you happily answer: "I'm working on my *NP-N120*?"

Chances are high you wouldn't. If you did your friend might think you were either high or a serious *Star Wars* fan.

On the other hand if you have an ASUS *Eee PC,* chances are higher you would mention: "Oh, I'm working on my *Eee PC*".

Not only because the name is memorable, but especially because it's easy to use.

Another example is Lycos versus Google. Which one is easier to tell your friend? You can answer by looking at which company is bigger nowadays. Google has become even famous as a verb "let me *google* it…" or "I've just *googled*…" have become quite common.

The added benefit of course is that the easy-to-use name often stirs up some word of mouth, which you wouldn't mind, would you?

6. Legal

Lastly, you want to check the legality of using the name. Is someone else already using the name (which would mean that unknowingly you would be stealing)? To check this, you can simply consult your intellectual property lawyer for confirmation.

Great Innovators follow the GUMSEL principle when choosing a name for their product or service. They make sure the name is globally usable, unique, memorable, short, easy-to-use and legal.

Innovation into Action

What is the name of your product or service?

_____

Check it based on GUMSEL (and if necessary rethink it):

Global _____

Unique _____

Memorable _____

Short _____

Easy-to-Use_____

Legal _____

Attractive Packaging

"Make it simple. Make it memorable. Make it inviting to look at. Make it fun to read."

Leo Burnett, Advertising Pioneer

Do you judge a book by its cover?

If you said no, you're in a distinct minority. The truth is that even though we've all been taught not to judge a book by its cover, the majority of us do so anyway.

In the following section I will share with you how to create better packaging for your product or service.

Like it or not, people DO judge a book by its cover.

For Product innovations

When we talk about packaging, we talk about everything except the product itself.

This includes to some degree also the exterior design.

For example, if you want to buy a BMW you will be offered the 'sports package' for several of their cars.

The 'sports package' is a simple package that makes the car look sportier, more special and ultimately more expensive.

For Service innovations

If you have to innovate on a service, you might think you don't need proper packaging.

But you couldn't be more wrong.

If you are in the service business, you need even better packaging.

Let's for example say that you own a chain of restaurants. What do you need to consider in terms of packaging? Well, here are just a few things:

- interior design that goes with your overall branding strategy

- the color and fonts of your menu

- the logo of the sign hanging over the entrance

- your brochures and printed marketing material

- in some cases, the marketing messages on both the inside and outside of your shop

- and the list goes on

We could make the same case for fitness clubs, accounting firms, etc.

When it comes to packaging your product or service, you need to consider the following six things:

1. Color

What colors best represent your product or service? Color experts will tell you that certain colors evoke certain emotions and that certain colors will attract a certain type of clientele.

Color	Meaning
Blue	Trustworthy, calming, dependable, committed
Green	Tranquil, refreshing, peaceful, ecological
Yellow	Optimistic, enlightened, happy, positive
Red	Exciting, dangerous, passionate, high emotion

You might want to research more colors than the above list, but this is a good start.

Which color matches the image of your product or service best?

Write it down here: _____

2. Fonts

Fonts matter!

The Apple logo has a modern look. It also has a modern font (Myriad).

Mercedes Benz

The Mercedes Benz logo has a traditional look. It also uses a traditional font (close to Times New Roman).

The fonts you put on your packages convey a certain meaning and feeling to the buyers of your product or service.

There are tens of thousands of fonts nowadays with more created daily, so it's sometimes hard to choose which font to use.

To give you just one example for choosing the right font:

There are **Serif Fonts** Vs. **Sans-Serif Fonts**. Serif Fonts have a more old-fashioned, traditional look to them, whereas Sans-Serif Fonts look more modern.

So, depending on your product or service you can choose from either category.

For example, if you plan to launch a website like Wikipedia that deals with information from the past, you want to go with a more traditional font.

On the other hand, if you plan to launch a new website like GQ online that talks about future global fashion trends, you might want to go with a modern font (Sans-Serif Fonts).

And if you plan to create a website for kids, then you might want to go with more playful fonts.

Also, for your packaging you need to consider if you are going to:

a. Choose 1 or more fonts

b. Use the same font for the logo and other text, or mix them up

A website that has lots of great fonts which I recommend you check out is: www.fonts.com. You can find lots of different font categories under "Classification" from 'Famous Fonts' to 'Technical Fonts' to 'Scary Fonts' to 'Graffiti Fonts' to 'Handwritten Fonts' and so on.

Just keep one thing in mind: choose fonts based on the image of your product or service that you wish to portray. Choose fonts based on the emotion you want to evoke in your end users.

Which fonts best match your products or services:

List them here:

_____

3. Pictures & Images

High-quality pictures and images can help you sell your product or service more easily.

What's on the Fiji Water bottle? Images of Fiji.

Celebrities or models on products have constantly outsold the competition, not just because of the celebrity effect, but also because pictures and images are simply more attractive.

What pictures and images can you add to your product/service to make it more attractive?

List some ideas here:

_____

_____

4. Size (e.g. memory sticks)

What size will your packaging be?

In general the bigger the size of the packaging, the more customers agree to pay more.

Don't believe me?

Check the packaging of the last USB stick you bought.

Even though the USB stick itself was probably tiny, the packaging was gigantic.

USB packaging is usually about 10 times the size of the real product. The are many other products and services that offer big size for higher price.

An even better example was the Hyundai Platinum credit card delivered to my friend last month. The packaging for the tiny card was incredible: It was about the size of a small notebook computer.

Even better, Hyundai Card delivered its platinum card using a delivery man dressed in a black suit with white gloves and handed the "card" (it's packaging was the size of a big notebook) over to my friend with both hands and a bow. How's that for packaging and showing the product's "value"?

The question YOU need to consider is: How big will your packaging be?

List some of your ideas here:

_____

5. Shape

A Coca Cola bottle has the shape of a woman.

What shape will your packaging have?

Will your packaging be round or square?

Round has a friendlier, younger, more casual feel to it.

Cornered has a sharper, stronger, more official feel to it.

There is no right or wrong. Again, everything is based on who the user is and what image your product should convey.

What will be the shape of your packaging?

List some of your ideas here:

_____

6. Negative Space

Last, but not least, you need to consider negative space.

The easiest way to explain negative space is by imagining an empty room.

Imagine the following scenarios in that empty room:

a. only one chair in the middle of the room

b. too many chairs in the room, so full that it seems cramped

c. about the right amount of chairs; not too much space, not too little space

The space around the chairs is what's called "negative space".

In case a. we have lots of negative space, in case b. very little, and in case c. we have a well balanced amount of negative space.

Which one would you prefer for your packaging?

Again, that depends on your product!

In general it is best to use images and words that leave a well-balanced amount of negative space.

When images and words are packed too closely together, your packaging ends up overwhelming the user and makes it difficult for them to take in your brand identity.

Too much negative space makes some people feel that something is missing or that the product is incomplete.

There are some cases where little or lots of negative space are good, but in general you should go with a well-balanced amount of negative space.

Great innovators create attractive packaging.

Innovation into Action

What packaging do you want to create? Or, how would you like to improve on your current packaging? Describe details here:

_____

_____

_____

_____

_____

_____

Client Testimonials

"Google actually relies on our users to help with our marketing. We have a very high percentage of our users who often tell others about our search engine."

Sergey Brin, Google Co-founder

"WOW! Your new product is amazing! I love the upgraded design and how easy it is to use. Thanks to the new features I can now save more than an hour a day while still getting the same results. Highly recommended!" – Tom Cooper

What would you think if you read the above about a product you're considering buying?

Chances are you would be quite persuaded by the REAL testimonial.

Testimonials, reviews, feedback, praise, and the like sell products and services much better, not to mention faster.

YOU can BRAG about your product or service all you want, but it's nothing compared to when YOUR USERS brag about your product or service.

THEIR feedback is thousands of times stronger than your created marketing messages to get potential buyers to buy your product or service.

Use testimonials extensively!

> # Clients that BRAG about your product or service are the clients that will make you the most money.

Companies like Apple, Google, BMW, Guinness, Bang & Olufsen, etc. have some of the most loyal customers out there.

These customers naturally BRAG about the company to anyone they meet or spread the messages online or in print.

You also want to use your loyal customers to your advantage using testimonials.

Testimonial Types

1. Written Testimonials

The first type of testimonials (and the easiest to get and use) is written testimonials.

This type of testimonials can be used on your website, in your brochures, on your packaging, in your sales letters, in your newsletters, in your emails to your subscriber list, on your office walls (for other clients to see), and so on.

Written testimonials work best the more of the following you can get from the person giving you the testimonial: (a) exciting testimonial, (b) picture, (c) full name, (d) job position, (e) company name, (e) location (this one is optional). The more the better.

Below is an example of a strong testimonial:

> "Product XYZ has made an incredible impact on my life. Ever since I started taking XYZ daily my energy has doubled. I feel healthier and stronger."
>
> Michael Schmidt
> Vice President
> Health Science AG
> Berlin, Germany

2. Sound-Recorded Testimonials

The second type is sound-recorded testimonials. This type is of course mainly broadcast via radio or online radio. The benefit is that it's easier to convey the EMOTION of the testimonial via voice recording versus just the written message. The downside is that your clients cannot SEE anything. So, let me share with you the third type, which can be the most effective one...

3. Video-Recorded Testimonials

The third type is video-recorded testimonials. These are probably the best to use.

Video testimonials can be used on your website, in your online newsletter (embedded), circulated on websites like www.youtube.com, and so on.

Also, TV commercials that include testimonials can work very well.

The more information you can get for your testimonial, the better.

4. Word-of-Mouth and Word-of-Mouse Testimonials

Actually the best way to spread all 3 testimonial types above is to use viral marketing.

Viral marketing means that users or clients tell one another about a product or service that they have used and liked. They can either do that in person using word-of-mouth, or online using word-of-mouse (spreading emails, writing online about your product or service or putting videos of it all over the internet, so others can easily find it).

Word-of-Mouth and Word-of-Mouse testimonial marketing can be one of the most effective ways for you to get the word out about your product or service fast.

Types of testimonials

Just as it is important what type of testimonials to use, it is also important WHO actually gave the testimonial. So let's have a look at different types of people who supply you with testimonials.

1. Normal users

Normal users are regular users who love your product or service and are willing to give you their testimonial in writing. This can be truly anyone who uses your product or service.

2. Expert testimonials

Expert testimonials are testimonials given by experts in your industry. They can include (but are not limited to) authors, doctors, famous speakers, bloggers or other famous people from your product or service's industry.

For example, most business books get testimonials from CEOs, other authors, or high level experts. Getting testimonials from Warren Buffet or Bill Gates or Lee Iacocca or Steve Jobs, etc. can help boost book sales.

Authors in the field of self-help that appear on Oprah or novelists getting their books into Oprah's book club probably receive the ultimate testimonial.

3. Celebrity testimonials (paid)

Celebrity testimonials are everywhere - they're on TV, on the cover of magazines, on billboards, on the sides of bus stops, and on your cereal box. And 9 times out of 10, you'll end up having to pay for them.

A celebrity can be defined as a person who has a big followership (fans) in his or her field.

The rule of thumb is the more famous they are, the more out of pocket you will be.

Another rule of thumb is to what the celebrity is known for, for what you'd like your product to be known for. Here are some examples:

Sean Connery [Stylish] just recently did advertisements for Louis Vuitton.

Sarah Jessica Parker [Fashion-conscious] used to endorse GAP.

Chuck Norris [Active] has endorsed the total gym® for a long time.

Brad Pitt [Sexy] endorses TAG Heuer watches.

Tiger Woods [Sporty] endorses Nike Golf wear.

The above strategy is not only limited to big companies. Small and medium-size companies can also use local "stars" in a specific field to market their products or services.

For example the team that invented the Pushup Pro got Jack Zatorski, the 2003 pushup world champion to promote their product.

Which celebrity could you hire to endorse your product or service?

4. Celebrity testimonials (unpaid)

Unpaid celebrity testimonials can be the best of all. These are testimonials where celebrities out of their own choice market your product or service for you, simply because they like it or believe in it so much.

One company that has used unpaid celebrity testimonials extensively is Coffee Bean. Coffee Bean uses pictures of celebrities drinking their coffee all over Asia to promote their brand inside their shops.

When Paris Hilton wears Hello Kitty T-shirts or visits Hello Kitty stores in Japan (paparazzi take photos while she's shopping there, which get published in gossip magazines), all these represent unpaid celebrity testimonials for the Hello Kitty brand.

There are lots of ways to use testimonials to your benefit. Great Innovators use testimonials to their fullest extent.

Innovation into Action

Whose testimonials can you use or get?

_____

_____

_____

_____

_____

_____

Conclusion
The 2 Roads

Conclusion: The 2 Roads

We've come to the end of the book. But really your journey into innovation and creativity has just started.

You now have the tools and the system to create great products and services easier and faster and with a higher chance of success.

From here it's up to you.

You can pick one of two roads now.

The first road is to close this book and change nothing, do nothing.

If you go down this road, you might create "OK" products or services and you might sometimes think of this book as an "interesting read".

Ultimately though your chances of changing your clients' world and adding massive value to lots of ideal users will be minimal at best.

There is nothing wrong with this road. It's the road that most people take.

The second road is the one of extreme execution.

You don't just read this book.

You reference it…again and again and again.

You apply everything you learn here.

You learn more through your own experience.

You create products and services that make a difference.

You create products and services that ultimately change the world and make you feel proud of your creative and innovative abilities.

This is NOT the easy way!

It takes courage and passion and the will to create something great.

Most importantly it requires you to sometimes be very TICKED OFF with the status quo.

This road has far more Ups AND Downs.

This road is tougher and will make you face your fears in a way you (probably) haven't experienced before.

But ultimately when you break through and create something that makes a difference, the sweat and the tears and the worries will all have been worth it, because you and your team can taste the sweetness of success.

With that said, I dare you to choose the second road.

To your continued innovation success,

Ben A. Ratje

Seoul, South Korea

About the Author

Ben A. Ratje is the Kyobo bestselling author of 'Presentation Latte'. He is the founder and CEO of INFLUENCE7, a communications and innovation consulting firm serving FORTUNE Global 500 and other large corporations.

Ben is a serial entrepreneur who has owned business ventures in three different countries. He has an impressive track record of creating products and services, selling B2B, B2C and B2G. He currently owns three businesses.

Ben lives with his wife in Seoul, South Korea.

EDGE INNOVATION SERVICES

**For inquiries about innovation
training or consulting from
the author and his team
please visit:**

www.influence7.com

or E-mail:

info@influence7.com

Available Innovation Services

- Innovation Workshops (8-24 hours)
- Innovation Seminars or Speeches

www.ingramcontent.com/pod-product-compliance
Lightning Source LLC
Chambersburg PA
CBHW060333200326
41519CB00011BA/1924